Cambridge Elements ≡

Elements in Public Economics
edited by
Robin Boadway
Queen's University
Frank A. Cowell
The London School of Economics and Political Science
Massimo Florio
University of Milan

BEHAVIORAL SCIENCE AND PUBLIC POLICY

Cass R. Sunstein
Harvard University

CAMBRIDGE
UNIVERSITY PRESS

CAMBRIDGE
UNIVERSITY PRESS

University Printing House, Cambridge CB2 8BS, United Kingdom

One Liberty Plaza, 20th Floor, New York, NY 10006, USA

477 Williamstown Road, Port Melbourne, VIC 3207, Australia

314–321, 3rd Floor, Plot 3, Splendor Forum, Jasola District Centre,
New Delhi – 110025, India

79 Anson Road, #06–04/06, Singapore 079906

Cambridge University Press is part of the University of Cambridge.

It furthers the University's mission by disseminating knowledge in the pursuit of
education, learning, and research at the highest international levels of excellence.

www.cambridge.org
Information on this title: www.cambridge.org/9781108972789
DOI: 10.1017/9781108973144

First published 2020

A catalogue record for this publication is available from the British Library.

ISBN 978-1-108-97278-9 Paperback
ISSN 2516-2276 (online)
ISSN 2516-2268 (print)

Behavioral Science and Public Policy

Elements in Public Economics

DOI: 10.1017/9781108973144
First published online: October 2020

Cass R. Sunstein
Harvard University
Author for correspondence: csunstei@law.harvard.edu

Abstract: Behavioral science is playing an increasing role in public policy, and it is raising new questions about fundamental issues – the role of government, freedom of choice, paternalism, and human welfare. In diverse nations, public officials are using behavioral findings to combat serious problems – poverty, air pollution, highway safety, COVID-19, discrimination, employment, climate change, and occupational health. Exploring theory and practice, this Element attempts to provide one-stop shopping for those who are new to the area and for those who are familiar with it. With reference to nudges, taxes, mandates, and bans, it offers concrete examples of behaviorally informed policies. It also engages the fundamental questions, including the proper analysis of human welfare in light of behavioral findings. It offers a plea for respecting freedom of choice – so long as people's choices are adequately informed and free from behavioral biases.

Keywords: behavioral economics, welfare, freedom of choice, government, public policy

ISBNs: 9781108972789 (PB), 9781108973144 (OC)
ISSNs: 2516-2276 (online), 2516-2268 (print)

Contents

1 Introduction

The topic of this Element is human welfare and how to improve it. To explore that topic, it will be necessary to say something about freedom, choice, rationality, deprivation, and what makes for a good life. To do that, we must explore both theory and practice.

Behavioral science emphasizes how human beings depart from perfect rationality. The pertinent findings bear on pandemics, highway safety, immigration, poverty, climate change, discrimination, criminal behavior, employment, education, human rights, the rule of law, and much more. Armed with an understanding of how human beings actually behave, we can have a better sense of how to solve concrete problems. In many nations, this practice has gotten better. The list of nations that have used behavioral findings productively includes New Zealand, Australia, Germany, Qatar, Lebanon, Denmark, India, the United Kingdom, the Netherlands, Sweden, and the United States. In those nations, and many others, the practice will get better still. International organizations are also using behavioral science; a great deal of work is being done at the United Nations, the World Bank, and the World Health Organization.

At the same time, behavioral findings raise fresh questions about the relationship between people's choices and their welfare. How shall we answer those questions? That is one of my preoccupations here.

Spurred by the pathbreaking work of psychologists Daniel Kahneman and Amos Tversky, and then by economist Richard Thaler, behavioral economics has had a massive impact not only on academic research but also on private and public institutions of diverse kinds. Hospitals are enlisting behavioral insights to save lives and money; they are applying those insights to help not only patients but also doctors and nurses. Companies, both large and small, are using behavioral insights to gain customers and to do better by them. Colleges and universities are using behavioral economics to help students to do better (and to stay in school). Governments are using behavioral insights to address a wide assortment of problems. Social media companies, including Facebook and Twitter, are using behavioral insights for good (and sometimes for not-so-good). The list of applications is very long.

My main goal here is to provide one-stop shopping, via the following: (1) an introduction, above all for those interested in public policy, to the key behavioral findings; (2) a sense of what governments are doing (with particular emphasis on the United States, the nation that I know best, with the belief that the lessons are far more general); and (3) an exploration of the relationship between behavioral economics and human welfare. Much of the treatment will, I hope, be suitable for those who are new to the subject, or who want to know what all the shouting is about – or how behavioral insights might be enlisted in the coming years.

At the same time, those insights have spurred some important and unresolved debates about how to think about choice, freedom, and the role of the state. Such debates have been with us for a very long time (Aristotle, who appears in these pages, had many relevant things to say), but new findings raise fresh questions about fundamental matters. I aim to provide an organizing framework for thinking about the legitimate functions of government, the place of freedom of choice, and the vexed question of paternalism. As we shall see, there is a lot for government to do – and a lot for it not to do.

A note on terminology before we begin: The term "behavioral science" usually refers to three overlapping fields – cognitive psychology, social psychology, and behavioral economics. Cognitive psychology explores how the human mind works. How do people decide whether a risk is high or low, and whether we should do anything about it? Social psychology explores the effects of social interactions. How do group interactions affect people's assessment of whether a risk is high or low, and whether it makes sense to try to take precautions against it? Behavioral economics engages in economic analysis with an understanding of how human beings actually behave. How might biased assessments of risks explain the movements of stock prices? How might limited attention account for the terms we observe in mortgages, school loans, and contracts between credit card companies and their customers?

The term "behavioral insights," often used in government circles, refers to behavioral findings from all of these fields. The term "behavioral welfare economics" refers to efforts to analyze human welfare in light of behavioral findings; it is one of my main topics here.

The term "welfare" has diverse meanings in diverse fields, and we will encounter what seem to be the principal alternatives here. In my preferred understanding, the term refers to the kinds of lives that people live; people have more welfare if they live better lives. "Welfare" includes how much people enjoy their days, how much they suffer, and to what extent they feel that their lives are meaningful and worthwhile. This conception of welfare is associated with the thinking of Jeremy Bentham and John Stuart Mill; with Mill, and against Bentham, I mean to understand the idea as going beyond pleasures and pains (though they certainly matter). But this is not a work of philosophy, and it will be sufficient, for my purposes, to show that people's choices often decrease their welfare; that allocative efficiency, as understood in economics, is not equivalent to welfare, as it ought to be understood, even within economics; and that a broader understanding, focused on the kinds of lives that people live, will lead both theory and practice in productive directions.

2 The Behavioral Revolution

Many people have been interested in increasing consumers' use of "green energy" – energy sources that do not significantly contribute to air pollution, climate change, or other environmental problems. Green energy sources, such as solar and wind, are available in numerous places, but in some nations relatively few people have chosen them even when it is fairly easy to do so. This is true notwithstanding the fact that in response to survey questions, many people insist that they would choose green energy.

In Germany, as in most nations, the use of green energy sources was very low for a considerable time. But even in a period of low use, in the 1990s and early 2000s, two communities in Germany did show strikingly high levels of green energy use – in one period, well over 90 percent. This was a dramatic contrast to the level of participation in green energy programs in most other cities in Germany, which in the same period was minuscule (around 1 percent). What is the reason for the difference? The answer is simple: in those two communities, people were automatically enrolled in green energy programs and they had to opt out (Pichert and Katsikopoulos, 2008).

All over the world, influential people in government and the private sector are becoming increasingly aware of the power of default rules. In part as a result, automatic enrollment in green energy is now widespread in Germany. All over the country, consumers are not opting out (Kaiser et al., 2020). The environmental benefits are significant. For those who are concerned about air pollution, climate change, and related problems, a new policy tool is on the agenda, and it is highly effective (Ebeling and Lotz, 2015): automatically enroll people in green energy, and let them opt out if they prefer.

Decades of work in behavioral science have shown that human beings are not perfectly rational (Pohl, 2016). Human beings tend to show "present bias": today and tomorrow really matter, but the future is a foreign country, Laterland, which we cannot be sure that we will ever visit. People may suffer from "internalities" (Farhi and Gabaix, 2020); they might impose costs on their future selves (as, for example, by smoking or by failing to protect their health). We are "loss averse"; a loss from the status quo makes us sadder than an equivalent gain makes us happy. A small fee for using a plastic bag at a convenience store may have a considerable impact in reducing the use of plastic bags (Homonoff, 2018).

On average, people tend to be unrealistically optimistic. In many ways, this is good, but it can make us unwilling to take precautions – for example, against dangers to our health. (In extreme cases, unrealistic optimism can fuel a pandemic.) We are not always good at assessing risks. Inertia greatly matters;

if we are automatically enrolled in a plan of some kind, participation rates will be far higher than if we have to opt in, even if the costs of opting in are exceedingly low. The power of inertia helps account for the effects of automatic enrollment in green energy.

All of these findings matter to public policy, and in recent decades, governments have taken notice of them. They have used behavioral insights to combat poverty, to promote public health, to reduce highway deaths, to respond to the COVID-19 pandemic, to fight discrimination on the basis of race and sex, and to reduce the risks associated with air pollution and climate change. Prominent practitioners of behavioral science can be found in governments all over the world, including the United Kingdom, the United States, the Netherlands, Canada, India, Ireland, Germany, Australia, Sweden, Brazil, India, Qatar, Saudi Arabia, the United Arab Emirates, and New Zealand. They can also be found in international organizations, including the World Bank, the World Health Organization, and the United Nations, all of which have made meaningful use of behavioral findings.

Nudges and Well Beyond Nudges

Return for a moment to the example of green energy defaults in Germany. If a green default rule is in place, people are being *nudged* (Thaler and Sunstein, 2008). A *nudge* is defined as an intervention, from either private or public institutions, that affects people's behavior while fully maintaining their freedom of choice. A GPS device is a canonical example. It tells you what route to take and thus helps you get where you want to go – but you specify the destination, and you can reject its advice and take your own route if you prefer. A default rule is a nudge, so long as you can easily opt out. The same is true of warnings and disclosure of information.

Other nudges include reminders, simplification of forms, increases or decreases in portion sizes, choice of colors for products, and decisions about the order in which items are placed on a website, ballot, or menu, or in a cafeteria. Some institutions, including some governments, emphasize social norms or widespread social practices; they are nudging. The response to the COVID-19 pandemic of 2020 included a great deal of nudging – for example, in New Zealand, Australia, and India. In the United States, the Credit Card Accountability Responsibility and Disclosure Act of 2009 contains an assortment of nudges, involving disclosure and default rules, as well as behaviorally informed mandates and bans. In India, the ambitious effort to improve public health by eliminating open defecation has included a large number of nudges, informed by behavioral economics.

Some nudges, such as disclosure of information, are educative. Other nudges are not educative; they change the architecture (such as default rules, or placing healthy foods in a more prominent place in grocery stores). Some nudges, like green energy defaults, are principally designed to prevent harm that choosers might inflict on others. Other nudges, like reminders that bills are due or automatic enrollment in pension plans, are principally designed to prevent harm that choosers might inflict on themselves.

It is important to emphasize that *nudges are just one tool in the behavioral toolbox*. Behavioral insights can also support the use of more coercive approaches, such as taxes (including those on cigarettes and sugar-sweetened sodas). Behavioral insights can also support the use of subsidies (such as for antismoking campaigns and for electric cars). Mandates and bans might have a behavioral justification. If people are required to buckle their seat belts, wear motorcycle helmets, or save for retirement, or if a nation imposes fuel-economy or energy-efficiency requirements, it might be because of an understanding of people's imperfect choices, stemming from unrealistic optimism, limited attention, or present bias. This is so even if we are judging people's welfare by reference to their own commitments and values (Le Grand and New, 2015). As noted, governments might attempt to improve people's welfare by protecting their future selves (the case of "internalities").

Much of the time, nudges are complements to mandates and bans, rather than substitutes. People might be prohibited from engaging in certain acts but also nudged to comply with the law. A fuel-economy mandate might be accompanied by fuel economy labels, encouraging people to buy the most fuel-efficient cars. During the COVID-19 pandemic of 2020, many governments mandated certain actions (such as wearing masks in public places) but also nudged people to do as the mandate required. Some antismoking policies are bans (such as the prohibition of smoking in public places), but others are nudges (such as graphic warnings, directly informed by behavioral economics).

I will return to the uses of coercion in due course. Eschewing coercion, nudges count as *libertarian paternalism*, an admittedly unlovely term that is no oxymoron. They are libertarian because they preserve freedom of choice. They are paternalistic insofar as they reflect a judgment, by those who select them, about what would promote the welfare of the people whom they affect – with welfare (again, and importantly!) defined by those people themselves (Le Grand and New, 2015; Sunstein, 2014). A GPS device helps people get where they want to go. If people want to go to a street in London, it does not direct them to a street in Oxford instead. It remains true that some of the most important behaviorally informed policies are mandates and bans, but because they preserve freedom of choice, nudges have important advantages.

By definition, nudges do not include criminal penalties, civil penalties, taxes, or subsidies. However, it should be immediately apparent that the idea of "maintaining freedom of choice" is ambiguous. A small fine or subsidy does not eliminate freedom; people can pay the fine or forgo the subsidy. In this light, it is more precise to define a nudge as an initiative that affects people's behavior without imposing significant material burdens or offering significant material benefits. As an economic incentive approaches zero, it starts to look more like a nudge. A tiny subsidy is an economic incentive, but it might reasonably be admitted to the family of nudges. It is also true that nudges can impose significant psychological or other nonmaterial costs; consider graphic health warnings or nutritional labels, which might make people scared or sad. A full accounting of the costs and benefits of nudges, and of their effects on people's welfare, should include those emotional costs (Sunstein, 2020).

Some people have an aversion to nudges, and we will discuss their objections in due course. But it is important to see that a certain amount of nudging is inevitable, because people's decisions are made against a background established by a society's *choice architecture.* Just as a building cannot lack an architecture, so a society cannot lack a choice architecture. A cafeteria has to have some kind of order for its items (cake first, or fish first, or vegetables first?). No grocery store, coffee shop, computer store, or rental car store can avoid creating an architecture that will influence people's choices. A website has an architecture too, and its display will influence what people select. Facebook, Instagram, Twitter, and YouTube are well-aware of this fact. They are alert to behavioral economics, they use behavioral insights, and they do plenty of nudging.

Whenever a product comes in a color or shape, and whenever there is music or instead silence, people's choices may well be affected. Any disclosure policy has to be framed in some way (does it emphasize potential losses or potential gains?), and the frame will influence decisions. Doctors and lawyers frame options, and hence they nudge. Whenever a default rule is in place – and it is usually hard to operate without default rules – nudging is involved. (To be sure, *active choosing*, an important kind of choice architecture, might dispense with default rules.)

The good news is that once we appreciate the power of nudging, we will see that inexpensive and seemingly modest initiatives can have large and highly beneficial effects in areas that include health, medical care, smoking, energy, education, the environment, savings, and much more (Benartzi et al., 2017). A central goal is to supplement the conventional set of policy instruments by identifying new tools (Thaler and Sunstein, 2008; Johnson and Goldstein, 2013;

Chetty et al., 2014). In addition to the energy use example with which I began, consider just a few illustrations:

- Automatic enrollment in retirement plans has been found to have a larger impact on savings than significant tax incentives (Chetty et al., 2014).
- Efforts to simplify federal financial aid forms have been found to have the same effect on college attendance as a several-thousand-dollar increase in the level of the subsidy (Bettinger et al., 2009).
- A social norms approach to energy conservation, informing people of how their energy use compares to that of their neighbors, has had the same impact in reducing energy use as an 8–20 percent short-term increase in the price of electricity (Allcott, 2011b).
- A simple change in the default rule for printing, from single-sided to double-sided, has been projected to have a far more substantial effect in reducing total paper usage than a 10 percent tax on such usage (Sunstein and Reisch, 2014), which means that indifference can make the world greener (Egebark and Ekstrom, 2016).

There are many other examples. As noted previously, behavioral insights have helped spur the use of taxes, subsidies, mandates, and bans. Soda taxes and cigarette taxes are an especially interesting example; one of the goals here is to protect people from their own mistakes.

Humans and Econs

The argument for nudging, or for other uses of behavioral economics in policy, can depend on a simple lack of information. If people do not know how to get where they want to go, a nudge might help. But the argument is also fortified by decades of evidence, specifying how people's judgments go wrong. Behavioral scientists, most prominently Daniel Kahneman in his masterful book on the topic, have distinguished between two families of cognitive operations in the human mind: fast and slow (Kahneman, 2011). *Fast thinking*, often called System 1, is rapid, automatic, emotional, and intuitive. *Slow thinking*, often called System 2, is slow, calculative, and deliberative. In many situations, System 1 does not err. But if we want to know what to do in unfamiliar or complex situations, System 1 may be unreliable. If it is working well, System 2 is a terrific safeguard. The label "Econs" has been used for those who act in accordance with System 2. Those who are influenced by System 1 count as "Humans" (Thaler and Sunstein, 2008).

Many behavioral findings can be organized with this framework. Because of the power of System 1, humans can be myopic and impulsive, giving undue weight to the short-term (perhaps by smoking, perhaps by texting while driving, perhaps by refusing to wear a mask during a pandemic, perhaps by eating too much; Laibson, 1997). Humans procrastinate and sometimes suffer as a result (O'Donoghue and Rabin, 2001; Thaler and Benartzi, 2004). They can be unrealistically optimistic and for that reason make unfortunate and even dangerous choices (Sharot, 2011). What is *salient* greatly matters (Bordalo et al., 2012a; Bordalo et al., 2012b).

People's ignorance of "shrouded attributes" (such as late fees or overuse charges) often stems from limited attention (Gabaix and Laibson, 2006). If an important feature of a situation, an activity, or a product lacks salience, people might ignore it, possibly to their advantage (perhaps because it is in the other room, and fattening) and possibly to their detriment (if it could save them money or extend their lives). Importantly, Humans make "affective forecasting errors": they predict that activities or products will have certain beneficial or adverse effects on their own well-being, but those predictions turn out to be wrong (Dunn et al., 2011; Gilbert, Pinel, et al., 1998). (I will return to this point in Section 3.)

Humans also use well-known heuristics, or mental shortcuts, in assessing risks, and even though they generally work well, those heuristics can lead in the wrong directions. For example, people err because they use the *availability heuristic* to answer difficult questions about probability. How likely is a terrorist attack, a hurricane, a traffic jam, an accident from a nuclear power plant, a case of venereal disease, a pandemic? When people use the availability heuristic, they answer a question of probability by asking whether examples come readily to mind. They are not exactly irrational to do so, but as a result, they can make serious errors. They can be too fearful – or too complacent.

3 Do Our Choices Make Us Happy?

Many of us assume that people's choices generally make them happy, or at least make their lives go better by their own lights. If people choose hamburgers rather than hotdogs, it is probably because they like hamburgers more than hotdogs. And if they choose veggie burgers instead, it is either because they prefer the taste of veggie burgers or because they have moral qualms about eating animals. It is tempting to believe that people's choices provide excellent evidence of what will promote their welfare – including, as part of their welfare, all of their concerns. Much of the time, the belief is right. But some of the time, it is not.

The goal of this section is to explain that claim, with reference to the most important behavioral findings. As we will see, some of those findings bear directly on what private institutions should be doing and also on the role of government.

The starting point is that when making a choice at one time, people tend to make predictions, or forecasts, about how they will feel about their choice at some later time. Think of these as "welfare forecasts." (I will occasionally use words like "happy" and "happiness" here, but what really matters is welfare, not happiness; as we will see in Section 7, people often choose options that make their lives better, in terms of what matters to them, even if those options do not, strictly speaking, make them "happier.") Serious errors in welfare forecasting can be demonstrated in several ways: by comparing people's welfare forecasts with direct measures of welfare, such as whether they are financially better off (assuming that this is what matters to them, in context); by creating situations in which people's choices lead to lower levels of subjective well-being and demonstrably worse experiences, by their own lights, when those too are what they care about; and by showing that people's welfare forecasts are influenced by factors that are clearly irrelevant on any account of what is relevant.

Consider the example of John Jones, a very hungry Human (he missed lunch) doing his weekly shopping at a grocery store late one Monday afternoon. Suppose that Jones's current state of intense hunger leads him to buy an overly large dinner portion to eat later in the week, on a day when he will eat his normal lunch at the office. If so, Jones has made a forecasting error that has led to a bad choice. Such forecasting errors can arise for a variety of reasons. Much welfare forecasting is done by System 1 rather than System 2, and for that reason, welfare forecasts are susceptible to the biases found in other intuitive judgments.

Daniel Kahneman and Shane Frederick (2002) have argued that a process of *attribute substitution* is involved in many of the heuristics that govern intuitive thinking. The argument is relevant to theory and practice alike; it bears, for example, on health, safety, and discrimination on the basis of race and sex. When people confront a hard question, the answer to a related but easier question will often come to mind first. People may adopt the accessible answer as the desired one without ever becoming aware that the wrong question has been answered. Consider the availability heuristic: people answer the question of whether a risk is worth worrying over by asking whether they can think of a situation in which the risk has come to fruition. The intuitive answer may go terribly wrong.

Welfare forecasts suffer from similar problems. The choices of the shopper who salivates at the sight of enticing food items may express his current hungry state, rather than a dispassionate prediction of his appetite on Thursday evening. If the circumstances differ between the time of choice and the time of experience, judgments and decisions that reflect the state at the time of choice may well turn out to be biased and hence erroneous.

To be clear, the claim is not that people do not know what they like. They do when the experience immediately follows the choice and when the experience is familiar: we are rarely surprised by the taste of the second spoonful from a bowl of soup. But people do not always know what they *will* like, and they are most likely to err when the temporal gap is long and when the agent's state and circumstances vary between the time of choice and the time of experience.

Four areas of errors in welfare forecasting have been well-documented: (1) when people try to forecast their future adjustment to new life circumstances; (2) when the emotional or motivational state of the agent is very different at the time of choice and the time of experience; (3) when the nature of the decision focuses attention on aspects of the outcome that are not actually that important, overall; and (4) when choices are made on the basis of flawed evaluations of past experiences. How these findings bear on what governments should do is a fair question. But if we are asking about the relationship between people's choices and their welfare, the findings offer significant cautionary notes. I draw here in part on laboratory and experimental evidence, but the same findings have been found in the field – that is, in actual life.

Mispredicting Adaptation

Often people must assess the effect of a long-term change in life circumstances. Recall that social psychologists Daniel Gilbert and Timothy Wilson coined the term "affective forecasting" to describe this mental activity (2000). Many of the changes that people make in their lives are driven by the wish to improve their happiness or reduce their unhappiness, or otherwise to improve their welfare, and inevitably those changes are based on some ideas about the actual effects of these circumstances. People have strong intuitions about the effects on their well-being of being rich or poor, obese or athletic, old or young, healthy or sick. People also forecast the happiness or misery of acquaintances who marry, of couples who divorce, of professors who get tenure and others who do not, of people who move from the Midwest to California, or others who move in the opposite direction. These intuitions and forecasts may be relevant to decisions about jobs, marriage, divorce, and moving to California. As Gilbert and Wilson noted, mistakes of affective forecasting can cause bad choices, which they call "miswanting" (Gilbert and Wilson, 2000).

The central result of many explorations of affective forecasting has been described as a "focusing illusion," which Kahneman has described with a simple maxim: "Nothing in life matters quite as much as you think it does while you are thinking about it" (Schkade and Kahneman, 1998). In other words, human beings show a powerful tendency to exaggerate the importance of any aspect of life when they focus their attention on it. This bias is easily explained. The task of evaluating the impact of a change in life circumstances inevitably draws attention to the distinctive aspects of the change. For example, thoughts about weather and climate are very likely to be salient in considering a move to California, or in evaluating a proposition such as "people are happier in California." But this selective focus is likely to bias judgments. When you focus on a particular aspect of a situation, you might neglect the possibility that you will not so much focus on that aspect in the future.

Indeed, a focusing illusion has been found in an investigation of just this question: Would you be happier if you lived in California? David Schkade and Daniel Kahneman (1998) polled students at two large Midwest universities and two large Southern California universities. The students were asked a series of questions about life satisfaction, either about themselves or "a student with your values and interests" at one of the other universities. Respondents in both California and the Midwest believed that students in California would be significantly happier, yet self-reported life satisfaction was virtually identical in the two locations.

The explanation is straightforward: When asked to report on their well-being, people normally focus on the central aspects of life, such as their health and their relationships, and usually do not pay a lot of attention to the climate. When they try to imagine the happiness of someone in a different location, however, the dimensions on which the regions differ will loom large. Climate is therefore far more important in affective *forecasts* than in actual well-being – hence the bias.

The focusing illusion helps resolve two central puzzles in the study of well-being (Ubel et al., 2005). The first puzzle is that people often adapt surprisingly well to important changes in their lives, even such dramatic changes as becoming a paraplegic or winning the lottery. (But this is imperfect; in terms of life satisfaction and subjective well-being, it is not good to become a paraplegic and it is good to win the lottery. But the effects are not as large as people expect.) These events may have large immediate effects on well-being or misery, but the biggest effects tend to be short-lived; paraplegics are rarely miserable a year after becoming paraplegic, and lottery winners are not especially happy a year after winning the lottery.

The second puzzle is that the first should be surprising at all. Although adaptation is ubiquitous, it is poorly represented in the naïve theory of well-being from which affective forecasts are drawn. Unless they know a paraplegic personally, for example, people make similar predictions of the mood of a paraplegic, regardless of whether they were told that the individual had been paralyzed for only a month or for a whole year. The same insensitivity to time is observed when respondents predict the mood of lottery winners. Here again – unless they know a lottery winner personally – people predict the same general level of euphoria for lottery winners, a month or a year after the event.

Notably, the pattern of responses is quite different for people who have personal knowledge of paraplegics (Schkade and Kahneman, 1998). Personal knowledge is not a significant factor in predictions of the *initial* misery of paraplegics – it is reasonable to suspect that these predictions are fairly accurate. However, only the better-informed respondents know that the initial misery would largely dissipate within a year of the event.

Withdrawal of attention is a main mechanism of adaptation to life changes such as becoming a paraplegic, becoming suddenly wealthy, or getting married (Ubel et al., 2005). Attention is normally associated with novelty. Thus the newly paraplegic, lottery winner, and newlywed are almost continuously aware of their state. But as the new state loses its novelty, it ceases to be the exclusive focus of attention, and other aspects of life again evoke their varying hedonic responses. Research indicates that paraplegics are in a fairly good mood more than half the time as soon as one month after their crippling accident (ibid.). Intuitive affective forecasts will miss this process of adaptation, unless they are corrected by specific personal knowledge.

Gilbert and Wilson have conducted a systematic program of research on biases of affective forecasting, in which they report several demonstrations of *duration bias*, which is their label for people's tendency to overestimate the power of adaptation. In a typical study, Gilbert, Pinel, and their colleagues (1998) interviewed current and former junior faculty members at the University of Texas. The current assistant professors were asked a series of fourteen "life satisfaction" questions ("In general, how happy are you these days?") and then were also asked about how happy they would be at various stages of their life in the event that they were either given or denied tenure. Former assistant professors – some of whom had been promoted, others denied – were also polled about their happiness. These were pooled into two groups: those whose tenure decision was within the past five years, and those for whom it had been from six to ten years ago.

Current junior faculty members think that tenure will make them very happy in the short run (the first five years) and somewhat less happy thereafter. They also think that getting denied tenure will make them quite miserable during the first five years, though they expect to be pretty well recovered after that. However, actual reactions during the first five years after the tenure decision – both favorable and unfavorable – were far milder than anticipated. Gilbert and his coauthors report similar biases in forecasts about the impact of success or failure in other domains, from dating to the outcome of a political election or a major sporting event. The conclusion from this body of research is that people are systematically wrong in their expectations about the life circumstances that will increase or decrease their happiness, which in turn implies that life choices that people make in their pursuit of happiness are also likely to be wrong (Wilson and Gilbert, 2003).

I have noted that happiness is not all that matters; people might sacrifice some smiles for a sense of meaning. But in the cases under discussion, happiness is a significant part of what matters to people, and they are mistaken about what will or will not make them happy.

Our Biased Learning from the Past

Consumers' choices often involve experiences they have already had, as in visiting a restaurant with a familiar menu. When people decide on the basis of personal memories, they will probably like what they choose. Choices from a familiar menu do not yield many surprises. However, welfare forecasts that are based on memories of past encounters will be biased if these memories are themselves biased – and several sources of such biases have been established.

No less than forecasts of the future, evaluations of the past are anchored on the individual's emotional state when the evaluation is made. In addition, our overall evaluations of extended outcomes systematically overweight some parts of the experience and underweight others. Biased evaluations of past episodes have been documented in a series of early experiments in which participants reported retrospective evaluations of experiences that varied in both the type of experience and its duration – for example, pleasant or horrific films, annoyingly loud sounds, and painful medical procedures (Schreiber and Kahneman, 2000). In most of these experiments, the participants also provided a continuous or intermittent report of the quality of their current experience by using a joystick or answering periodic questions.

One of the strongest findings of these experiments was that retrospective evaluations of episodes were radically insensitive to the length of time subjects were exposed to the stimulus. This is called *duration neglect* (Kahneman et al., 1993). Essentially, people's retrospective evaluations of both pleasant and unpleasant experiences can be explained not by the length of time but by a *peak/end rule* – a simple average of the quality of the experience at its most extreme moment and at its end predicted retrospective evaluations with great accuracy (ibid.).

The peak/end rule violates an elementary principle of rational evaluation, which asserts that increasing the duration of a painful episode makes things worse, not better. By the peak/end rule, however, extending a period of pain can improve its remembered welfare if the peak is unchanged and the new end is not as bad as the original. To demonstrate this result, Kahneman and his colleagues paid experimental participants to undergo three trials of an experience called the cold-pressor, in which a hand is immersed to the wrist in painfully cold water and kept there until the experimenter announces that it may be removed. The first two trials were conducted as follows (Kahneman et al., 1993). In the short trial, a hand was immersed in water at 14°C (57°F) for 60 seconds. (This may not seem very cold, but think about going into the ocean off the coast of Maine and you will get the idea.) In the long trial, the hand was also immersed at 14°C (57°F) for 60 seconds, and then over the next 30 seconds, the temperature was gradually raised to 15°C. The two trials were separated by seven minutes, and their order was varied across subjects.

The participants continuously indicated the intensity of the pain they experienced, using a joystick. The mean of reported pain intensity in both conditions was 8.4 on a scale of 0–14 after 60 seconds, which is when the short trial ended. When the long trial ended, mean reported pain was only 5.8 – still somewhat painful but a distinct improvement of the peak/end average.

Seven minutes after the second trial, each participant was asked to choose which of the two experiences would be repeated for the third trial. Overall, 22 of 32 participants elected to repeat the long trial, which exposed them to 30 seconds of pain they could have avoided. The proportion of choices of the long trial was 80 percent (17/21) among the participants who indicated diminishing pain during the last 30 seconds of that trial. The remaining 11 participants, who had indicated no change in pain, divided their choices about equally between the long and the short trial. Both results are predicted by the peak/end rule.

Similar behavior has been observed in other settings. For example, a clinical trial of colonoscopy was conducted in which half the patients were randomly exposed to a condition in which their colonoscopy was extended by keeping the instrument stationary for about a minute before removing it (Redelmeier et al., 2003). The extra period was uncomfortable but not very painful. Believe it or not, this manipulation resulted in a big improvement in people's retrospective judgments of the pain of the procedure – and in an increase in the number of repeat colonoscopies that people would be willing to undergo within the subsequent five years.

In these experiments, people are not deliberately choosing to have more pain rather than less. Indeed, they recognize that in principle, less pain is better than more, and they would conform to that principle if their attention were appropriately directed. Not surprisingly, participants prefer the short cold-pressor trial over the long one when the two trials are verbally described. It is when people choose on the basis of their memories that they get in trouble – because their preferences reflect the neglect of duration as a factor in the evaluation of past episodes. We need far more evidence on the question of whether and when people's choices are mistaken because they are based on their memories. But there is no doubt that such mistakes occur.

Our Current Emotional State

The case of John Jones, the hungry shopper, illustrates a proposition that has been explored in numerous studies: people's forecasts of how they will feel in the future are greatly affected by how they feel in the present. The outcome has been labeled a "projection bias" (Loewenstein et al., 2003), since people are projecting their current mental state onto a future one. A fun (or is it alarming?) example is the "hot-cold empathy gap" (Loewenstein, 2005). When aroused – by hunger, sex, or anger – people mispredict how they will think and behave in a "cool" state, and when cool, they mispredict the effects of being aroused. In both situations, they underestimate the impact of a change from their current state.

The hungry shopper is not hypothetical. It is well established that shoppers who are hungry tend to buy food as if they expected to remain permanently famished (Nisbett and Kanouse, 1968), but shoppers who are given a muffin to eat before entering the supermarket are more likely to restrict their shopping to the items on their list (Gilbert, Gill et al., 1998). The effect is easily explained: the attractiveness of food increases with current hunger. Of course, the delicacy (or bag of potato chips) that appears irresistibly wonderful to the hungry shopper may have lost much of its charm when it is consumed later. Similarly, a study found that telephone catalog shoppers were overly influenced by the current weather when shopping and prone to buy items they will not want later (Colin et al., 2004). For example, warm clothes purchased on very cold days are more likely to be subsequently returned.

The projection bias makes it more likely that people will not like what they choose. And if people's current state affects their decisions, they will make related blunders as well. Consider the purchase of membership in health clubs. The health benefits are the focus of attention at the time of purchase, but other considerations are likely to be more salient when the question is whether to visit the club on any given occasion. The failure to anticipate these shifts of salience may contribute to many purchases of memberships by people who later make little or no use of them (DellaVigna and Malmendier, 2006).

More generally, some virtuous choices that people make may involve a lack of sufficient empathy for the future self who will have to live with the choice – and who will decline to do so. In an elegant demonstration of this phenomenon, Daniel Read and his colleagues (1999) provided people with coupons that allowed them free rental of several films. Films of two types were available: some were edifying or "highbrow" (like *Schindler's List*) while others were lowbrow and fun (*Sleepless in Seattle*). The films were to be available either for the same evening or for the next day. People tended to select lowbrow movies for viewing tonight and highbrow movies for tomorrow. (Are you surprised?) People's desire to improve their minds, and to learn something, is apparently more salient when choosing a movie for later – while the desire to relax and to have fun is more salient when choosing for the very near future.

The Power of Context

A good may be evaluated in explicit comparison with other goods or on its own. People's preference for one or another good may be different when the two are compared explicitly to each other or evaluated separately, perhaps by willingness to pay or by a rating. Chris Hsee (2000) has established a key mechanism that produces such reversals of preference: people may notice subtle differences between goods (like two shades of purple) when the goods are directly compared, but they may fail to detect the same differences when the goods are evaluated separately. In joint evaluation, some characteristics of goods are salient even though they are irrelevant in separate evaluation (Sunstein, 2018b).

Here's a simple example: Would you rather have a dictionary with 100,000 words and a torn cover, or a dictionary with 50,000 words and an intact cover? Comparing the two dictionaries directly, most people will choose the bigger one. But evaluating the two dictionaries separately, people will pay more for a smaller dictionary with an intact cover than for a larger one whose cover is torn. For current purposes, the key point is that people might choose a good (such as a radio, a cell phone, or a car) in joint evaluation, even though they will experience it in separate evaluation – and may therefore end up having an inferior experience.

Hsee (2000) offers a compelling thought experiment to illustrate the point. Imagine that you are in the market for stereo speakers and you are comparing various models at the home audio store. You narrow your choice down to two similarly priced models, A and B. The A speakers sound somewhat better than the B speakers, but they are quite ugly. Which do you choose? At the store you engage in joint evaluation, comparing one model against another. In the store, your attention is likely to be focused on the quality of the sound, and you may assign considerable weight to small differences in this attribute. But your task is to predict the welfare you will get from the speakers when you listen to music at home. At home, there will be just one set of speakers, so you will be performing a separate evaluation. Small differences in sound quality will not be noticeable without a standard of comparison. In contrast, comparison is not required to evaluate whether an object is ugly or beautiful. People are therefore susceptible to the mistake that Hsee described – paying too much attention to the small (but noticeable *in the store*) difference in sound quality, and too little attention to appearance.

Comparative effects can arise even when the task does not explicitly require it. Volunteers in a study conducted by Morewedge and colleagues (2010) were asked to predict how much they would enjoy eating potato chips a few minutes later. In one experimental condition, subjects could also see a chocolate bar next to the potato chips; in another condition, the chocolate was replaced by a tin of sardines. The irrelevant foods influenced the participants' predictions of their future enjoyment, which was much reduced by the presence of the chocolate (sensibly enough, if people prefer chocolate to sardines). The prediction was comparative, although no comparison was required. Eventual enjoyment of the chips, however, was completely unaffected by the irrelevant food that remained on the table. The experience of eating is focused on the food we actually consume and is not dependent on the options we turn down.

A different type of discrepancy between the context of choice and the context of experience arises when people make a simultaneous choice about goods that will be consumed sequentially. An admittedly dated example is the choice of which CDs to load into the stack of a CD player (Read et al., 2001). In making the decision at a single time, people focus on the attribute of variety that seems desirable (in the case of CDs, variety of singers or types of music). However, the variety of a sequence is usually less important in the experience of consumption. As a consequence, people often choose more variability than they will actually enjoy.

In the first demonstration of this phenomenon, Itimar Simonson (1990) conducted an experiment on the students in two of his classes. In a brilliant move to increase his teacher ratings, he promised to bring the students snacks for three consecutive weeks. The students had to decide which snacks they wanted from a menu of six snacks, ranging from Snickers bars to bags of potato chips. The only difference between the setup for the two classes was that the students in one class (the simultaneous-choice group) chose all three snacks during the first session, while the students in the other class (the sequential-choice group) chose a single snack in each session. Simultaneous-choice subjects typically took a different snack for each class, while sequential-choice subjects often wanted the same snack every time. It is a good guess that the sequential-choice choosers enjoyed their snacks more.

This study shows what Daniel Read and George Loewenstein call the *diversification bias*: namely, the tendency for people to choose *too much* variety. The term implies that sequential choice leads to greater experienced welfare. This prediction was confirmed in several studies in which participants reported their enjoyment of decisions made either simultaneously or sequentially. For example, participants in a study by Read et al. (2001) chose two audio tracks (music or comedy), either sequentially or simultaneously. They chose more variety in simultaneous choice, but they enjoyed high-variety sets less than low-variety ones.

Of course, it is true that people care about others; they want to act morally. And when people choose, their own well-being may not be the only or even the central question. But much of the time, people are trying to make choices that will, on average, make them as well off as possible. The problem is that to undertake this task, people must start by making a forecast about how the various possible outcomes will be experienced. And if their forecasts are systematically biased, their choices may fail to make them better off. In numerous cases, forecasts of future welfare turn out to be biased (Sunstein, 2018b). I will return to this problem in Section 6. For the moment, let us focus on how governments use behavioral science.

4 Government

I have noted that all over the world, behavioral science in general, and nudging in particular, have been attracting high-level attention (Halpern, 2015; OECD, 2010). Both the developed and the developing world are seeing opportunities. With respect to new policy initiatives, developments have been proceeding at an exceptionally rapid pace, so much so that any account will rapidly become out of date.

In Canada, the United States, Germany, Japan, Australia, New Zealand, Sweden, Denmark, the Netherlands, Qatar, and the United Arab Emirates, important initiatives enlist tools such as disclosure, warnings, and default rules, and they can be found in multiple areas, including fuel economy, finance, energy efficiency, environmental protection, highway safety, smoking, health care, and obesity (with behavioral findings playing an unmistakable role in efforts to improve diet). As a result, behavioral findings and nudges have become important reference points for regulatory and other policy making in multiple nations.

Some of the most prominent efforts can be found in the United Kingdom. Those efforts began in 2010 under former Prime Minister David Cameron, who created a Behavioural Insights Team, sometimes described as "the Nudge Unit," with the specific goal of incorporating an understanding of human behavior into policy initiatives. In its early years, the official website stated that its "work draws on insights from the growing body of academic research in the fields of behavioural economics and psychology, which show how often subtle changes to the way in which decisions are framed can have big impacts on how people respond to them" (Cabinet Office, n.d.).

Now partly private, the Behavioural Insights Team has become far more ambitious. It is working in more than thirty nations. It has used behavioral insights to promote initiatives in numerous areas, involving smoking cessation, energy efficiency, organ donation, consumer protection, employment, crime, sex equality, COVID-19, and compliance strategies in general. Other nations have expressed keen interest in the work of the Team, and its operations are continuing to expand. In 2012, the United States created its own behavioral insights team, and many other nations have now done so, including (for example) Australia, Singapore, the Netherlands, Germany, Canada, Qatar, Lebanon, Saudi Arabia, India, and Japan.

It is important to note that most of the world's behavioral work is undertaken by departments and ministries that have a large repertoire of responsibilities, and that are not dedicated "behavioral teams." For example, I worked in the White House under President Barack Obama, as Administrator of the Office of Information and Regulatory Affairs. We drew heavily on behavioral findings, working with the Department of Transportation, the Environmental Protection Agency, the Social Security Administration, the Department of the Treasury, the Department of Health and Human Services, and many more. Something similar can be said of many nations, including Germany, Denmark, and Canada.

Behavioral economics has drawn considerable attention in Europe as a whole. Early on, the Organisation for Economic Development and Cooperation (OECD) published a Consumer Policy Toolkit that recommends a number of initiatives rooted in behavioral findings (OECD, 2010). In the European Union, the Directorate-General for Health and Consumers has also shown the influence of behavioral economics (DG SANCO, 2010). A report from the European Commission, called *Green Behavior*, enlists behavioral economics to outline policy initiatives to protect the environment (European Commission, 2012; iNudgeYou.com, n.d.). Private organizations are also using behavioral insights to promote a variety of environmental, health-related, and other goals (see inudgeyou.com, n.d.; greeNudge.org, 2018). As I have noted, important work has been undertaken at the United Nations, the World Bank, and the World Health Organization.

In the United States, regulatory efforts have been directly informed by behavioral findings, and behavioral science has played an unmistakable role in the design of important laws, including the Credit Card Accountability Responsibility and Disclosure Act, the Affordable Care Act, and the Dodd-Frank Wall Street Reform Act (Sunstein, 2013). Indeed, something very close to the idea of nudging is built directly into a prevailing Executive Order on regulation, which amounts to a kind of mini-constitution for the regulatory state: "each agency shall identify and consider regulatory approaches that reduce burdens and maintain flexibility and freedom of choice for the public. These approaches include warnings, appropriate default rules, and disclosure requirements as well as provision of information to the public in a form that is clear and intelligible" (Executive Order 13563, 2011). Executive Order 13707 is even more explicit, calling out "behavioral science insights" in plain terms and directing agencies to consider those insights (Executive Order 13707, 2015).

It is clear that behavioral findings are having a large impact on regulation, law, and public policy all over the world. That impact is likely to grow over the next decades. Notably, the use of behavioral findings cuts across conventional political divisions, and tends to appeal to people with diverse views in diverse nations. In my own experience in the White House, most nudges did not divide people along political lines (although almost everything else did). Because behavioral findings suggest the possibility of low-cost, high-impact interventions (Benartzi et al., 2017), they are especially likely to attract considerable attention in economically challenging times.

Feast

Behavioral findings proved especially relevant to efforts to combat the COVID-19 pandemic of 2020. In responding to the pandemic, behavioral economics and nudging were broadly appealing and came into widespread use – not only by governments but also by private institutions, including hospitals, universities, and ordinary businesses, large and small. Those social distancing markers, indicating where people should stand in line? They are nudges.

To organize these and other efforts, a simple framework can be captured in an acronym: FEAST. The idea builds on the EAST framework from the Behavioural Insights Team (Behavioural Insights Team, 2014). EAST refers to four ideas: easy, attractive, social, and timely.

The first idea is that if you want people to do something, make it easy for them. They have to know what to do and how to do it, and doing it should not be too burdensome, painful, or costly. Automatic enrollment significantly increases participation rates simply because people do not have to exert effort to enroll. Whenever the goal is to change behavior, the best question is often overlooked: *Why are people not doing it already?* After getting the answer, public officials, employers, schools, and others can take steps to remove the barrier.

If we focus on E, we might think that the preferred approach is straightforward: make it automatic. And if that is not possible, the second best is also simple: make it easy. A striking example of the effect of automaticity, referred to previously, is the default setting on printers: if the setting is double-sided, people will use a lot less paper (Egebark and Ekstrom, 2016).

A corollary is that a good way to discourage people from doing something is to make it hard. In behavioral science, the term "sludge" is used for frictions, or administrative burdens, that make it difficult for people to get a license, a job, a permit, or benefits of various sorts (Sunstein, 2019d; Sunstein 2020). Sludge is sometimes necessary or good – for example, to ensure that the people who receive benefits are actually eligible. But sludge is often a curse, seriously harming people, including the most vulnerable.

It matters whether an option or message is attractive. A simple and vivid communication has more impact than a dull and complicated one. With respect to COVID-19, officials in Ireland have made excellent use of this insight with striking informational signs. The same is true of New Zealand. (Of course, it is also true that sometimes warnings should not exactly be attractive; they should be vivid. Graphic health warnings are an example.)

As we have seen, people also tend to be affected by what most other people do; hence the S for social in EAST. Notifying people of the actions of the majority can be a powerful nudge. We have seen that if people learn that they are conserving less energy than other people, they start to conserve more energy (Allcott, 2011b). Publicizing a current norm can greatly alter behavior. There is also evidence that even if a norm is not yet current, but is *emerging*, publicizing that fact can be effective (Sparkman and Walton, 2017). It is worth underlining that finding. When people learn that other people are increasingly engaging in certain behavior, they are more likely to do it, even if it has not yet attracted majority support (ibid.). This might be true in the domain of exercising, healthy eating, mask-wearing, or environmentally friendly behavior.

Timing is everything. Often it is best to provide people with information (including warnings) right before they make a decision, not the night before or when their minds are focused elsewhere. In the context of COVID-19: When nations started to relax stay-at-home orders and business shutdowns, they probably did best if they arranged health-related messages so that people saw them immediately before they made health-related choices. For example, such messages might be provided in grocery stores, including social distancing signals that give people general reminders and also guidance about where to stand in line.

For policy makers all over the world, EAST has proven useful. But it is missing something essential – fun. Hence my modest, behaviorally informed amendment, adding the F for FEAST.

How do you encourage people to eat more vegetables? A Stanford University study tried two different methods (Turnwald et al., 2019). The first involved labels that emphasized health benefits. The second used labels that emphasized enjoyment and taste. Both worked, but enjoyment proved to be the more powerful motivator. The health-focused labels increased vegetable consumption by 14 percent, which is a large improvement. The enjoyment-focused labels increased vegetable consumption by 29 percent, which is a terrific improvement.

Behaviorally informed marketers are keenly aware of the importance of enjoyment and fun. For example, Amazon sells certain products with what it calls "Frustration-Free Packaging." That means that there is not much in the way of plastic, wiring, or cardboard to deal with. Better still, Frustration-Free Packaging also turns out to be Green Packaging; it contains less solid waste, and the materials are recyclable. The company is making a smart behavioral bet, which is that the idea of Frustration-Free Packaging will make customers smile – and attract a lot more of them than would be motivated by the idea of sustainability.

No one thinks that a pandemic is fun. But if they are alert to behavioral findings, leaders can produce a sense of optimism, unity, hope, and more than a few smiles instead of despair, anger, division, and fear. Prime Minister Jacinda Ardern of New Zealand even managed to have some fun with the lockdown, describing the Tooth Fairy and the Easter Bunny as "essential workers," legally authorized to carry on their work. In general, New Zealand succeeded in meeting the pandemic not only with firmness, calmness, and determination but also with wit, a call to unity (emphasizing that the nation is "a team of five million"), and a consistent sense of good cheer. Its mantra has been "Be kind."

For many social problems, including public health, the most important parts of the FEAST framework have been the E for easy and the S for social. Complexity and confusion are mortal enemies of public health; good norms are its best friends. But here is a plea to leaders at all levels, even in dark times: Do not neglect the F. Human beings need it.

Institutionalizing Behavioral Insights: Two Approaches

What is the best method for implementing behavioral insights? It is certainly possible to rely entirely on existing institutions. We could imagine a system in which an understanding of behavioral science is used by current officials and institutions, including leaders at the highest levels. For example, the relevant research could be enlisted by those involved in promoting competitiveness, environmental protection, public safety, consumer protection, and economic growth – or in reducing private and public corruption and combating poverty, infectious diseases, mental health problems, and obesity. Focusing on concrete problems rather than abstract theories, officials with well-established positions might be expected to use that research, at least on occasion. (Leaders of private institutions could do the same thing.)

If those officials have both knowledge and genuine authority, they might be able to produce significant reforms, simply because they are not akin to a mere research arm or a think tank. Even a single person, if given the appropriate authority and mission, could have a large impact. On one model, the relevant officials would not engage in new research, or at least not in a great deal of it. They would build on what is already known (and perhaps have formal or informal partnerships with those in the private sector who work on these issues). In an important sense, this approach is the simplest because it does not require new offices or significant additional funding, but only attention to the relevant issues and a focus on the right appointments. In Canada, Sweden, Denmark, Germany, and the United States, this kind of approach has proved highly successful, with the adoption of many behaviorally informed reforms. In my years in the White House, I followed this approach, working in an existing institution (the Office of Information and Regulatory Affairs) relying on existing behavioral research.

A quite different approach would be to create a new institution – such as a behavioral insights team or a "nudge unit" of some sort. (Recall that this has been done in the United Kingdom, the United States, Australia, Germany, the Netherlands, Japan, Qatar, India, and increasingly many nations.) Such an institution could be organized in different ways, and it could have many different forms and sizes. On a minimalist model, it would have a small group of knowledgeable people (say, five), bringing relevant findings to bear and perhaps engaging in, or spurring, research on their own. On a more ambitious model, the team could be larger (say, thirty or more), engaging in a wide range of relevant research. A behavioral insights team could be created as a formal part of the government (the preferred model, to ensure real impact) or could have a purely advisory role.

Whatever its precise form, the advantage of such an approach is that it would involve a dedicated and specialized team, highly informed and specifically devoted to the relevant work, and with expertise in the design of experiments. If the team could work with others to conduct its own research, including randomized controlled trials, it might be able to produce important findings (as has, in fact, been done in the United Kingdom, Australia, and the United States, with similar efforts occurring elsewhere). The risk is that such a team would be akin to an academic adjunct, a kind of outsider, without the ability to power or ability to initiate real reform. Authority greatly matters. The United Kingdom has had the most experience with this kind of approach, and it has succeeded in part because it has enjoyed high-level support and access. In this domain, one size does not fit all, but it is noteworthy that a growing number of nations have concluded that it is worthwhile to have a dedicated team. Of course, the two approaches might prove complementary.

I now turn to a series of examples, with an emphasis on behaviorally informed policies now playing a role in public policy, particularly in the United States. As noted, I refer to efforts in that country only because of my own familiarity with them; similar efforts can be found in other nations.

Default Rules

Why They Matter

If there were an Olympic competition for behaviorally informed policy tools, default rules would win the gold medal. They often have very large effects (Jachimowicz et al., 2019), transforming outcomes in ways that combat poverty, improve the environment, increase savings, and protect consumers (ibid.). It is important to see that default rules can be used for good or for ill. If people are automatically enrolled in programs that do not help them, they might end up paying money for nothing at all (Luguri and Strahilevitz, 2019). It is therefore important to ensure that default rules are actually working to increase people's welfare.

A great deal of research has attempted to explore exactly why default rules have such a large effect on outcomes (ibid.; Gale et al., 2009; Dinner et al., 2011; Carroll et al., 2009). There are three major explanations (Jachimowicz et al., 2019; Johnson and Goldstein, 2013). The first involves *inertia and procrastination*. To alter the effect of the default rule, people must make an active choice to reject the default. In view of the power of inertia and the tendency to procrastinate, people may simply continue with the status quo. The second factor involves what might be taken to be an *implicit endorsement* of the default rule. Many people appear to conclude that the default was chosen for a reason; they believe that they should not depart from it unless they have particular information to justify a change. Third, the default rule might establish the *reference point* for people's decisions; the established reference point has significant effects because people dislike losses from that reference point (the behavioral finding of loss aversion). If, for example, the default rule favors energy-efficient light bulbs, then the loss (in terms of reduced efficiency) may loom large, and there will be a tendency to continue with energy-efficient light bulbs. But if the default rule favors less efficient (and initially less expensive) light bulbs, then the loss in terms of upfront costs may loom large, and there will be a tendency to favor less efficient light bulbs.

Consider in this regard the "endowment effect," which means that people value goods that they have more than they value the same goods when they are in the hands of others (Thaler, 2015). If, for example, you are given a coffee mug, a lottery ticket, or freedom from a risk, you will likely demand more to give it up than you would be willing to pay to get it in the first instance. The reasons for the endowment effect, and its boundary conditions, remain to be clearly established, but it appears to be produced in part by loss aversion: people are reluctant to give up what they have.

It is important to note that even if the effects of default rules are large, and they often are (Jachimowicz et al., 2019), they might not always be positive (Weimer, 2020). People might be defaulted into a pension plan, and many of them might benefit (and not opt out). But people might also be defaulted into such a plan, and some of them might lose, because they could use the money for something now (and even so, they might not opt out). If people are defaulted into a green energy plan, and if it is more expensive than a dirtier energy source, they might lose (and might not opt out). Because of the power of inertia, there is always a risk that a default rule will help some while hurting others. This is a point in favor of personalized defaults, a topic taken up below. And it strongly suggests a general point, which is that nudges should be subject to the same kind of welfare analysis as any other policy tool (ibid.). On net, are people being helped or hurt? Cost-benefit analysis is a standard way to answer that question, though it is far from perfect (Sunstein, 2020).

Savings

In many nations, employers have long asked workers whether they want to enroll in pension plans. Even when enrollment is easy, and even when the benefits of enrolling seem high, the number of employees who enroll, or opt in, has often been relatively low (Madrian and Shea, 2001; Gale et al., 2009). An increasing number of employers have responded by changing the default to automatic enrollment, by which employees are enrolled unless they opt out. The results are clear: significantly more employees end up enrolled with an opt-out design than with opt-in design (Gale et al., 2009). This is so even when opting out is easy. Importantly, automatic enrollment has significant benefits for all groups, with increased anticipated savings for Hispanics, African Americans, and women in particular (Orszag and Rodriguez, 2009; Papke, Walker, and Dworsky, 2009; Chiteji and Walker, 2009).

In Denmark, the large effects of automatic enrollment have been demonstrated with great rigor (Chetty et al., 2014). Indeed, the impact of automatic enrollment significantly exceeds the impact of tax incentives. The expensive option of tax incentives is far less effective than the cheap alternative of automatic enrollment. There is a general lesson here; sometimes nudges are far more effective than expected and indeed far more cost-effective than more familiar tools (Bernartzi et al., 2017).

In the United States, the Pension Protection Act of 2006 (PPA; Pension Protection Act, 2006) draws directly on behavioral findings by encouraging employers to adopt automatic enrollment plans. The PPA does this by providing nondiscrimination safe harbors for elective deferrals and for matching contributions under plans that include an automatic enrollment feature, as well as by providing protections from state payroll-withholding laws to allow for automatic enrollment. Building on these efforts, the Obama administration, with personal involvement from President Obama, undertook significant initiatives to encourage employers to adopt such plans, in part by making it easier for them to do so (Obama, 2009; Internal Revenue Service, 2009). An important part of automatic enrollment plans is *automatic escalation*, which can ensure that default contribution settings do not produce unduly low savings levels (Benartzi and Thaler, 2013).

School Meals

The National School Lunch Act (Healthy Hunger-Free Kids Act, 2012) takes steps to allow "direct certification" of eligibility, thus reducing complexity and introducing what is a form of automatic enrollment. Under the program, children who are eligible for benefits under certain programs will be "directly eligible" for free lunches and free breakfasts, and hence will not have to fill out applications (Healthy, Hunger-Free Kids Act, 2012). To promote direct certification, the USDA issued an interim final rule that was expected to provide up to 270,000 children with school meals (Department of Agriculture, 2011). The aggregate effects of direct certification are much larger, allowing participation by millions of additional children. According to recent counts, the number has been in the vicinity of fifteen million. It is worth pausing over that number.

Finance

Nudges, including default rules, are an important part of credit markets, and sensible nudging is doing a great deal to help consumers (Agarwal et al., 2013).

One example is the Federal Reserve Board's switch of the default rule, undertaken as part of its effort to protect consumers from high bank overdraft fees (12 C.F.R. § 205.17). To provide that protection, the Board issued a regulation in 2009, banning banks from automatically enrolling people in overdraft "protection" programs. Instead, customers have to sign up (12 C.F.R. § 205.17(b)). In justifying the regulation, the Board drew directly and extensively on the behavioral literature, with specific reference to the retirement issue (Willis, 2013; Sarin, 2019).

Interestingly, the available evidence, catalogued in an important article (Willis, 2013), suggests that the effect has not been as large as might be expected. The reason is that banks have used behaviorally informed strategies, including loss aversion, to encourage people to opt into the program in significant numbers. Nonetheless, large numbers of people are no longer enrolled in the programs (Sarin, 2019). The overall level of opt-in seems to be only around fifteen percent (Willis, 2013); to that extent, the opt-in default has been effective. Moreover, the largest proportion of people who opt in are those who actually go over their checking limits (Zywicki, 2013). For such people, it is not implausible to think that opting in is a good idea.

More generally, the bulk of the gains from the Credit Card Accountability Responsibility and Disclosure Act have come from behaviorally informed mandates and bans, targeting shrouded attributes such as late fees and overuse fees. It appears that these provisions are saving consumers over $11 billion annually, and the savings are concentrated among people with low credit ratings (Agarwal et al., 2013). There is a large lesson here as well. Under certain circumstances, bans on certain product attributes, if they are shrouded, can protect consumers (and also employees and investors) (Sarin, 2019).

Health Care

A provision of the Affordable Care Act (ACA) required that by a specific date, employers with over two hundred employees must automatically enroll employees in health care plans, while also allowing employees to opt out (Affordable Care Act, 2010). Another provision of the ACA was called the Community Living Assistance Services and Supports Act (CLASS Act, 2010); this provision created a national voluntary long-term insurance program. The ACA provided for an automatic enrollment system, whereby employers enroll employees in that program unless they opt out (CLASS Act, 2010). In addition, the ACA contains an automatic payroll deduction system for the payment of premiums.

On February 4, 2010, the Centers for Medicare and Medicaid Services (CMS) provided guidance to states via a State Health Official (SHO) letter (Centers for

Medicare and Medicaid Services, 2010). In cases where states are able to obtain all the information necessary to determine eligibility, the new option permits states automatically to enroll and renew eligible children in Medicaid or Children's Health Insurance Program (CHIP). This approach allows states to initiate and determine eligibility for Medicaid or CHIP without a signed Medicaid or CHIP program application, as long as the family or child consents to be enrolled in Medicaid or CHIP.

After enactment, these various provisions of the ACA were put under serious pressure, in part on political grounds; some of them were repealed. But their original enactment attests to the power of behavioral insights in national legislatures.

Payroll Statements

In 2010, the Department of Homeland Security changed the default setting for payroll statements to electronic from paper, thus reducing costs (Orszag, 2010). Many government agencies have done something similar. Changes of this kind will not exactly balance a nation's budget, but they can save significant sums of money for both private and public sectors.

Disclosure

Disclosure can take many forms, from the short and sweet to the long and sour. It can operate like a GPS device, telling people how to get where they want to go, or instead like a nightmare, leaving people badly confused. A great deal of work needs to be done to learn when disclosure is effective and exactly why (Sunstein, 2020). But there is no question that disclosure is proving to be an appealing nudge, and much of what has been done is behaviorally informed.

When disclosure requirements are imposed, it is often because less informed consumers are interacting with better-informed sellers and the incentives of the consumers and sellers seem to be misaligned. Consider, for example, interactions between an automobile seller and potential customer. The seller has better information about the safety of the cars it sells; the customer may have a greater interest in driving a safe car. Or consider interactions between a chain restaurant and its patrons. The restaurant has better information about the nutritional properties of the food it sells; the customer may have a greater interest in eating nutritious food.

There are also situations in which disclosure serves the purpose of helping to protect consumers against themselves. Some of these cases involve "behavioral market failures." Recall the concept of internalities (Farhi and Gabaix, 2020):

costs that individuals impose on themselves but fail to internalize at the time of decision. Smokers may enjoy smoking, but not so much lung cancer. Those who eat a lot of food and gain weight may love their meals, but not the health problems that come from them. Those who spend a lot of money today may not be so happy to find that they have nothing to spend tomorrow. Nudges can respond to the problem, and if they are behaviorally informed, they might stipulate format, framing, and other requirements that take account of cognitive and other factors in such a way as to make the relevant disclosure more effective.

Nutrition

In the domain of nutrition, a number of disclosure requirements are in place. For example, the US Department of Agriculture (USDA) issued a rule requiring the provision of nutritional information to consumers with respect to meat and poultry products. Nutrition facts panels must be provided on the labels of such products. Under the rule, the panels must contain information with respect to calories and both total and saturated fats (9 CFR § 317.309). The rule is behaviorally informed; it clearly recognizes the potential importance of framing. If a product lists a percentage statement such as "80% lean," it must also list its fat percentage ("20% fat"). This requirement should avoid the confusion that can result from selective framing; a statement that a product is 80 percent lean, standing by itself, makes leanness salient, and may therefore be misleading.

In a related vein, the USDA abandoned the Food Pyramid, used for decades as the central icon to promote healthy eating. The Pyramid was long criticized as insufficiently informative; it does not offer people with any kind of clear "path" with respect to healthy diet and does not connect to people's actual experience with food (Heath and Heath, 2010). In response, the USDA replaced the Pyramid with a new, simpler icon, the Food Plate, consisting of a plate with clear markings for fruit, vegetable, grains, and protein. The plate is accompanied by straightforward guidance, including "make half your plate fruits and vegetables," "drink water instead of sugary drinks," and "switch to fat-free or low-fat (1%) milk." This approach has the key advantage of informing people what to do if they seek to have a healthier diet. It is like a GPS device.

In 2014, the Food and Drug Administration proposed to improve and clarify the "nutrition facts" panel on most foods. The proposal is an unambiguous nudge, and it is behaviorally informed. Hence the FDA's explanation states:

> Changes in labeling may also assist consumers by making the long-term health consequences of consumer food choices more salient and by providing contextual cues of food consumption. We note that the behavioral economics literature

suggests that distortions internal to consumers (or internalities) due to time-inconsistent preferences, myopia or present-biased preferences, visceral factors (e.g., hunger), or lack of self-control, can also create the potential for policy intervention to improve consumer welfare … . Consistent with predictions based on models of bounded rationality, consumers can systematically make suboptimal dietary choices because they discount future health consequences relative to immediate benefits more than they would if they chose according to their underlying or true preferences, leading them to regret their decisions at a later date. To the extent that some form of intrapersonal market failure characterizes diet-related decisions, changes in labeling may assist consumers by making the long-term health consequences of consumer food choices more salient and by providing contextual cues of food consumption. (FDA, 2014)

The final version of the rule embeds these insights; there is no question that it is strongly influenced by behavioral findings.

Credit Cards

In the context of financial products, disclosure played a key role in the design of the Credit Card Accountability Responsibility and Disclosure Act (CARD), enacted in 2009. One of its provisions is a small nudge: every month, companies must disclose the interest savings from paying off the full balance within thirty-six months, instead of making only minimum payments every month. It is easy to be skeptical about disclosure requirements of this kind, but the consequence has been to reduce interest payments by $74 million a year – not a huge amount, but far from trivial (Agarwal et al., 2013).

As noted, the CARD Act contains other seemingly modest provisions designed to limit credit card fees. For example, companies are forbidden to impose fees on cardholders who go over their credit limit unless cardholders agree to opt in to authorize that practice. In addition, banks must give cardholders a forty-five-day advance notice of rate increases, and they must inform cardholders of their right to cancel the account before such increases go into effect.

These provisions have contributed to substantial decreases in both over-limit fees and late fees – with the overall package saving U.S. credit card users billions of dollars annually (Agarwal et al., 2013; Sarin, 2019). As noted, cardholders with low credit scores appear to be the biggest beneficiaries. To be sure, and importantly, the package includes behaviorally informed mandates and ban, significantly restricting late fees and overuse fees.

Health Care

The ACA includes a large number of nudges designed to promote accountability and informed choice with respect to health care. Indeed, ACA is, in significant part, a series of disclosure requirements, many of which are meant to inform consumers, and to do so in a way that is alert to behavioral findings. Under the ACA, a restaurant that is part of a chain with twenty or more locations doing business under the same name is required to disclose calories on the menu board. Such restaurants are also required to provide in a written form (available to customers upon request) additional nutrition information pertaining to total calories and calories from fat, as well as amounts of fat, saturated fat, cholesterol, sodium, total carbohydrates, and so forth (Affordable Care Act, 2010). There continues, of course, to be a dispute about the actual effects of disclosure requirements of this kind, and further evidence is indispensable (Sunstein, 2020; Bollinger et al., 2010; Downs et al., 2009).

In a similar vein, § 1103 of the Act calls for "[i]mmediate information that allows consumers to identify affordable coverage options." It requires the establishment of an Internet portal for beneficiaries to obtain easy access to affordable and comprehensive coverage options, including information about eligibility, availability, premium rates, cost sharing, and the percentage of total premium revenues spent on health care, rather than administrative expenses.

Implementing a provision of the ACA, HHS finalized a rule to require insurance companies to provide clear, plain language summaries of relevant information to prospective customers. The rule includes basic information, including the annual premium, the annual deductible, a statement of services that are not covered, and a statement of costs for going to an out-of-network provider. These are simply a few examples – the Affordable Care Act contains many others (Sunstein, 2011).

Fuel Economy

Automobile manufacturers have long been required to disclose the fuel economy of new vehicles as measured by miles per gallon (MPG). This disclosure is a nudge, and it helps promote informed choice. As both behavioral scientists and the Environmental Protection Agency (EPA) have emphasized, however, MPG is a nonlinear measure of fuel consumption (Environmental Protection Agency, 2009). For a fixed travel distance, a change from 20 to 25 MPG produces a larger reduction in fuel costs than does a change from 30 to 35 MPG, or even from 30 to 38 MPG.

Evidence suggests that many consumers do not understand this point and tend to interpret MPG as linear with fuel costs. If it occurs, this error is likely to produce inadequately informed purchasing decisions when people are making comparative judgments about fuel costs. Consumers tend to *underestimate* the cost differences between low-MPG vehicles and tend to *overestimate* the cost differences between high-MPG vehicles (Allcott, 2011a). By contrast, an alternative fuel economy metric, such as gallons per mile, could be far less confusing. Recognizing the imperfections and potentially misleading nature of the MPG measure, the Department of Transportation and EPA mandated a radically revised and behaviorally informed label, including a clear statement about anticipated fuel savings (or costs) over a five-year period (Sunstein, 2013).

Disclosure and Competition

If disclosure requirements are straightforward and simple, they should facilitate comparison shopping and hence market competition. Drawing directly on behavioral research, the Treasury Department's account of financial regulation emphasizes the value of requiring that "communications with the consumer are reasonable, not merely technically compliant and non-deceptive. Reasonableness includes balance in the presentation of risks and benefits, as well as clarity and conspicuousness in the description of significant product costs and risks" (Department of the Treasury, 2009). The department's analysis goes on to say that one goal should be to

> harness technology to make disclosures more dynamic and adaptable to the needs of the individual consumer. . . . Disclosures should show consumers the consequences of their financial decisions. . . . [The regulator] should . . . mandate or encourage calculator disclosures for mortgages to assist with comparison shopping. For example, a calculator that shows the costs of a mortgage based on the consumer's expectations for how long she will stay in the home may reveal a more significant difference between two products than appears on standard paper disclosures. (Department of the Treasury, 2009)

In keeping with this theme, the Consumer Financial Protection Bureau is authorized to ensure that "consumers are provided with timely and understandable information to make responsible decisions about financial transactions" (Dodd-Frank Act, 2010). The Bureau is also authorized to issue rules that ensure that information is "fully, accurately, and effectively disclosed to consumers in a manner that permits consumers to understand the costs, benefits, and risks associated with the product or service, in light of the facts and circumstances" (Dodd-Frank Act, 2010).

To accomplish this task, the Bureau is authorized to issue model forms with "a clear and conspicuous disclosure that, at a minimum – (A) uses plain language comprehensible to consumers; (B) contains a clear format and design, such as an easily readable type font; and (C) succinctly explains the information that must be communicated to the consumer" (Dodd-Frank Act, 2010; Riis and Ratner, 2015). In addition, the director of the Bureau is required to "establish a unit whose functions shall include researching, analyzing, and reporting on ... consumer awareness, understanding, and use of disclosures and communications regarding consumer financial products or services" and "consumer behavior with respect to consumer financial products or services, including performance on mortgage loans." Note that new technologies make it possible to inform consumers of their own choices and usages, an approach that may be especially important when firms have better information than consumers do about such choices and usages (Kamenica et al., 2011).

To the same end, the Department of Labor issued a final rule requiring disclosure to workers of relevant information in pension plans. The rule is designed to require clear, simple disclosure of information about fees and expenses and to allow meaningful comparisons, in part through the use of standard methodologies in the calculation and disclosure of expense and return information (29 CFR §§ 2550.404a-5). Evidence suggests that the rule, which was clearly informed by behavioral economics, has produced substantial savings for investors (Kronlund et al., 2020). In a similar action, the Department of Transportation required US air carriers and online travel agents to alter their web interfaces to incorporate all ticket taxes in upfront, advertised fares. Evidence suggests that this behaviorally informed intervention, designed to overcome shrouded prices, has been highly effective and thus saved consumers a lot of money (Bradley and Feldman, 2020).

Yet another example is provided by a final rule of the Department of Education that promotes transparency and consumer choice with respect to for-profit education by requiring institutions to provide clear disclosure of costs, debt levels, graduation rates, and placement rates (Department of Education, 2010a). These disclosures must be included "in promotional materials [the institution] makes available to prospective students" and be "[p]rominently provide[d] . . . in a simple and meaningful manner on the home page of its program Web site (34 CFR § 668.6; Department of Education, 2010b).

Structuring Choices

Complexity can also create problems through a phenomenon known as *choice overload*. In the traditional view, having more choices helps, and never harms, consumers or program participants. This view is based on the reasonable judgment that, if an additional option is not better than existing options, people will simply not choose it. In general, more choices are indeed desirable, but an increasing body of research offers qualifications, especially in unusually complex situations (Sethi-Iyengar, Huberman, and Jiang, 2004). For example, there is some evidence that enrollment may decline, and asset allocations may worsen (Iyengar and Kamenica, 2010), as the menu of investment options in a 401(k) plan expands.

Responding to this general problem in the context of prescription drug plans (Thaler and Sunstein, 2008), CMS took steps to maintain freedom of choice while also reducing unhelpful and unnecessary complexity (Gruber and Abaluck, 2011). The CMS Medicare Part D program rules require sponsors to ensure that when they provide multiple plan offerings, those offerings have meaningful differences. The rules also eliminate plans with persistently low enrollments, on the ground that those plans increase the complexity of choices without adding value (see also Korobkin, 2013).

Salience

It is often possible to promote social goals by making certain features of a product or a situation more *salient* to consumers. Increasing salience can be an effective nudge (Kronlund et al., 2020; Sarin, 2019). Consider the response to COVID-19, which consists in large part of making certain safeguards highly salient (staying home, washing one's hands, social distancing, wearing masks). Or consider alcohol taxes. There is evidence that when such taxes are specifically identified in the posted price, increases in such taxes have a larger negative effect on alcohol consumption than when they are applied at the register (Chetty, Looney, and Kroft, 2009; Finkelstein, 2009).

In the context of fiscal policy, there is a question whether to provide payments in the form of a one-time check or instead in the form of reduced withholding. Would one or another approach lead to increased spending? A one-time stimulus payment has been found to have significantly greater effects in increasing spending than does an economically equivalent reduction in withholding (Sahm, Shapiro, and Slemrod, 2011). A potential explanation, with support in the evidence, involves the importance of salience or visibility. Indeed, a majority of households did not notice the withholding changes in the relevant study, and households who found "a small but repeated boost to their paychecks" appear to be less likely to use the money for significant purchases.

A similar point applies in the domain of energy efficiency. For many consumers, the potential savings of energy-efficient products may not be salient at the time of purchase, even if those savings are significant. The "Energy Paradox" refers to the fact that some consumers do not purchase energy-efficient products even when it is clearly in their economic interest to do so (for a general framework, see Farhi and Gabaix, 2020). Empirical work suggests that nonprice interventions, by making the effects of energy use more salient, can alter decisions and significantly reduce electricity use. There is evidence that such interventions can lead to private as well as public savings (Howarth, Haddad, and Paton, 2000).

A related approach attempts to identify and consider the frame through which people interpret information. There is evidence that some consumers may not seriously consider annuities in retirement to insure against longevity risk – the risk that they will outlive their assets – because they do not fully appreciate the potential advantages of annuities (Brown, 2007). One hypothesis is that some people evaluate annuities in an *investment frame* that focuses narrowly on risk and return (Brown et al., 2008). Looking through such a frame, consumers focus on the risk that they could die soon after annuity purchase and lose all of their money. Some evidence suggests that efforts to shift consumers into a *consumption frame*, which focuses on the end result of what they can consume over time, help consumers appreciate the potential benefits of annuities (Brown et al., 2008). The goal here is not to suggest a view on any particular approach to retirement; it is merely to emphasize that the relevant frame can increase salience.

Social Norms, Safety, and Health

Behavioral scientists have emphasized the immense importance of social norms, which have a significant influence on individual decisions and thus operate as effective nudges. I have noted that when people learn that they are using more energy than similarly situated others, their energy use may decline – saving money while also reducing pollution (Allcott, 2011b). The same point applies to health-related behavior. It has long been understood that people are more likely to engage in healthy behavior if they live or work with others who so engage. And if people are in a social network with other people who are obese, they are significantly more likely to become obese themselves. The behavior of relevant others can provide valuable information about sensible or appropriate courses of action. Recall that if people learn about emerging norms, they are more likely to act in accordance with them, even if the majority does not yet do so (Sparkman and Walton, 2017).

These points have implications for policy. On October 1, 2009, President Obama issued an executive order that bans federal employees from texting while driving. Such steps can help promote a social norm against texting while driving, thus reducing risks. This same approach – emphasizing social norms – might be applied in many domains. In the domain of childhood obesity, for example, a social norm in favor of healthy eating and proper exercise could produce significant health benefits. Here, as elsewhere, public–private partnerships can play a key role, with those in the private sector helping to spur emerging norms that promote better choices by and for children.

In particular, the "Let's Move" initiative, designed to combat obesity, emphasized such partnerships and featured numerous nudges. First Lady Michelle Obama collaborated with Walmart to promote healthier choices (Mulligan, 2011). With respect to nudging, Walmart developed a "healthy seal" to help consumers to identify healthy choices. In a similar vein, a number of large food and beverage companies pledged to remove 1.5 trillion calories from their products by a specific date, in an effort to combat childhood obesity USA Today (May 21, 2010). Food Giants Pledge to Cut 1.5 Trillion Calories Out of Products. Retrieved from www.usatoday.com/money/industries/food/2010-05-17-cutting-calories_N.htm. The relevant steps include reduction of product sizes and introduction of lower calorie foods. The Food Marketing Institute and the Grocery Manufacturers Association agreed to promote informed choice through a "Nutrition Keys" label, designed in part to combat childhood obesity Food Market Institute. (October 27, 2010). Press Release: Food and Beverage Industry Launches Nutrition Keys, Front-of-Pack Nutrition Labeling Initiative to Inform Consumers and Combat Obesity. Retrieved from https://www.fmi.org/newsroom/news-archive/view/2010/10/27/food-beverage-industry-announces-front-of-pack-nutrition-labeling-initiative-to-inform-consumers-and-combat-obesity.

These are simply a few examples of efforts, ongoing all over the world, to use behavioral insights to promote public health. In the context of the COVID-19 pandemic, such efforts have been widespread. New Zealand repeatedly emphasized new norms consistent with protective behavior; something similar can be said about Australia, Germany, Ireland, and the United Kingdom. In the United States, Governor Jay Pritzker of Illinois launched an "All in Illinois" campaign that produced videos featuring celebrities encouraging residents to stay at home. The basic goal was to establish a new norm. Indeed, some of the successful responses to the pandemic represented a self-conscious effort to alter norms, informed by behavioral economics.

5 Mistakes

In Section 3, we saw that people sometimes make important mistakes, in the sense that their choices do not promote their welfare. Let us now broaden the viewscreen and address some fundamental questions.

For orientation, consider some hypothetical cases:

1. Sarah Masters recently bought a car. She considered a package with various safety features, including a camera designed to ensure rear visibility, but she rejected it; it would have cost $75. Many consumers are making the same decision that Masters made.

2. Jerry Lancaster is overweight (and as a result, at heightened risk of getting diabetes). He would like to diet, but he is not sure exactly how. He goes to restaurants every day for lunch, and he tends to order high-calorie items. He is not aware of the caloric content of his orders. Many consumers act as Lancaster does.

3. Pamela Harston is eligible for the Earned Income Tax Credit. She is aware of that fact. But she is not quite sure how to apply. She is also very busy. She thinks that she will apply next month. She has thought that for a long time. Many people are doing as Harston does: failing to apply for benefits for which they are eligible.

4. Edward Ullner is in his thirties; he is also healthy. In the midst of a pandemic, very much like the coronavirus pandemic of 2020, he is not especially worried. He does not believe that he will fall ill, and even if he does, he does not believe that he will suffer long-term harm. He does not wear a mask, and he does not stay at home.

In all of these cases, it is at least plausible to think that the relevant agent is making some kind of mistake – one that will produce serious harm. We could also believe, certainly in the case of Ullner, that harm to others is involved. But even if we bracket that possibility, the point remains: Ullner might be endangering his own life, perhaps because of an absence of information, perhaps because of unrealistic optimism. On welfare grounds, regulators might want to respond in some way, perhaps with a nudge, perhaps with an economic incentive, perhaps with a ban or a mandate (Farhi and Gabaix, 2020; Conly, 2013).

How should governments think about these issues? Should they be paternalistic? In what way and to what extent? I shall make two claims here. The first is that in light of behavioral findings, regulators should adopt a working presumption in favor of respect for people's self-regarding choices, but only if those choices are adequately informed and sufficiently free from behavioral biases (Le Grand and New, 2015). These are important qualifications, calling for significant departures from standard economic approaches to welfare analysis.

The second is that the working presumption is itself rebuttable on welfare grounds. Even if people's self-regarding choices involve their "direct" judgments (as defined later), regulators should not *necessarily* respect them. The particular means that people choose to promote their own ends might make their lives go less well, by their own account (ibid.). For example, they might die prematurely, or suffer from serious illness, and what they receive in return might not (on any plausible account of welfare) be nearly enough. The underlying reason might involve a lack of information or a behavioral bias, identifiable or not, in which case intervention can be made consistent with the working presumption; but the real problem might involve philosophical questions about the proper understanding of welfare, and about what it means for people to have a good life. Still, regulators should proceed with great caution, on the ground that reasonable people reasonably care about diverse goods, and they can make reasonable, and different, judgments about how much weight to give them. This point supports the working presumption and calls for humility in the face of self-regarding choices, certainly when choosers are sufficiently informed and sufficiently free from behavioral biases.

These points suggest that behavioral welfare economics, even as used in applied work and in government circles, must at least implicitly take a stand on the best understanding of welfare. I do not offer anything like a comprehensive account in this space, but in brief, I shall argue that

1. purely hedonic accounts, emphasizing pleasure and pain, ignore important aspects of what people legitimately care about;
2. preference-based accounts, emphasizing people's choices, pay too little attention to behavioral biases and also to the ingredients of what is, for essentially all people, a good human life; and
3. objective-good accounts tend to underplay human diversity, and the heterogeneous goods that matter to reasonable people.

The working presumption can be seen as a pragmatic way of accommodating points (1), (2), and (3). With respect to both theory and practice, it aspires to an "incompletely theorized agreement" (Sunstein, 2018a): a principle on which people can converge despite their disagreement or uncertainty about the most fundamental questions. It will be implicit that economic understandings of allocative efficiency, while useful and even important, fail to capture anything like a plausible understanding of welfare (Farhi and Gabaix, 2020).

We have seen that much of behavioral economics, and much of behaviorally informed analysis of law, focuses on departures from standard accounts of rationality (see Thaler, 2015 for a clear catalog). Exploring actual behavior, it seeks to avoid the most contentious normative questions about the relationship between choice and welfare. Those questions are very far from settled (Hausman and McPherson, 2009; Sugden, 2018). An illuminating and growing body of work explores whether and in what sense economists, lawyers, and others interested in behaviorally informed public policy can continue to insist on the sovereignty of individual preferences, while also acknowledging behavioral findings (for a highly selective account, see Allcott and Sunstein, 2015; Allcott and Kessler, 2019; Bernheim and Rangel, 2007, 2009; Bernheim, 2009; Gul and Pesendorfer, 2004; Farhi and Gabaix, 2020; Gabaix, 2019; Thunstrom, 2019). I shall argue for a degree of humility, captured in the working presumption in favor of respect for people's informed and behaviorally unbiased judgments (Allcott and Sunstein, 2015).[1] As we shall see, this presumption can be disciplined by asking a series of subsidiary questions, and it should be accompanied by a distinction between "means paternalism" and "ends paternalism," of special relevance to behaviorally informed law and policy (Le Grand and New, 2015; Acland, 2018).

Welfare, Sometimes

Do people's choices promote their welfare? As we saw in Section 3, the best answer is *sometimes*. If people lack information, they might choose poorly (Bar-Gill, 2012). If sellers exploit people's behavioral biases, consumers' choices may go awry (Akerlof and Shiller, 2016; Bar-Gill, 2012). We have seen that even without self-conscious exploitation of such biases, people may choose poorly because of limited attention, inertia, present bias (O'Donoghue and Rabin, 2015), or unrealistic optimism (Farhi and Gabaix, 2020; Gabaix, 2019; Sarin, 2019), potentially justifying a regulatory response of some kind (Bar-Gill, 2012; Farhi and Gabaix, 2020; Conly, 2013; Sarin, 2019).

As Section 3 also explained, people may make mistaken predictions about the effects of options on their welfare (Sunstein, 2019c). People are susceptible to supposedly irrelevant factors or "frames" (Keren, 2011; Scholten et al., 2019). We have seen that in an opt-in system, they might end up in a very different situation from where they end up in an opt-out system (Jachimowicz et al., 2019). If so, what is their preference (Goldin, 2015, 2017)?

In addition, people's preferences may be endogenous to legal rules and social norms (Mattauch and Hepburn, 2016); whether or not that that is so, preferences and values may shift over time, and choosers may not appreciate that fact ex ante (Ullmann-Margalit, 2006; Pettigrew, 2020). People sometimes "choose for changing selves" (ibid.). An enthusiastic meat eater might come to love salad and despise meat, in part because of learning, in part because of genuine preference change. These questions raise serious challenges for efforts to base law and policy on people's preferences, or to conduct any kind of welfare analysis on the basis of preferences. They help explain the growing effort in multiple fields to investigate subjective well-being, entirely unanchored in preferences (Dolan, 2014; Kahneman et al., 1997; Schkade and Kahneman, 1998; Adler, 2011; Bronsteen et al., 2013).

Return in this light to the cases of Masters, Lancaster, Harston, and Ullner. Masters might suffer from a lack of information or unrealistic optimism

---

[1] The presumption could be fortified with reference to the potentially self-interested or malevolent incentives of those who seek to interfere with people's judgments. I am bracketing that important point here.

(Sunstein, 2019b). Lancaster does not have important information; he might also have a self-control problem. Harston appears to be a procrastinator. Ullner lacks information as well; he might well be unrealistically optimistic. In all of these cases, some kind of regulatory intervention might increase people's welfare. If welfare is what we care about, we will not think that regulatory abstinence is mandatory.

Some of the most careful and illuminating discussions of the underlying issues, not yet engaged in law and policy, come from by B. Douglas Bernheim (2016), who begins by noting that "standard welfare economics" associates welfare with choices. We can understand Bernheim's work as the best and clearest effort to rescue the foundations of standard economic theory while acknowledging behavioral findings. (On the important issue of temptation and self-control, Gul and Pesendorfer [2004] is also particularly valuable.) Bernheim's work bears directly on questions in policy and law, such as the legitimate domain of paternalism, and for that reason, it is worth careful attention here.

Bernheim suggests that standard welfare economics invokes three general premises (Bernheim, 2016):

Premise 1: Each of us is the best judge of our own well-being.
Premise 2: Our judgments are governed by coherent, stable preferences.
Premise 3: Our preferences guide our choices: when we choose, we seek to
   benefit ourselves.

Something like these premises played a central role in the early decades of economic analysis of law (Posner, 1973), and they continue to play a significant role today. Bernheim (2016) recognizes that the resulting understanding "may fall short of a philosophical ideal" but urges that this "should not trouble us excessively," because it "captures important aspects of well-being and lends itself to useful implementation." That is an eminently reasonable claim, but it leaves open questions and it remains to be specified; in some cases, it might also point in the wrong directions. Consider, for example, the question of whether a soda tax is a good idea (Allcott et al., 2019); whether energy efficiency regulations can be justified as a response to consumer mistakes (Allcott, 2016); whether heavy taxes on cigarettes might make smokers better off (Gruber and Mullainathan, 2005; see also Farhi and Gabaix, 2020); whether motor vehicle safety regulation might provide people with "experience goods," such as rear visibility, and thus improve their lives by their own lights (Sunstein, 2019b); whether nudges or mandates might be a good idea in the context of a pandemic (to prevent harm to choosers, not to others). In these and other cases, falling short of a philosophical ideal might turn out to be a fatal flaw. Indeed, a significant soda tax seems to be a good idea on welfare grounds (Allcott et al., 2019).

And what, exactly, is meant by the claim that the standard understanding "captures important aspects of well-being"? Perhaps the suggestion, empirical in nature, is that much of the time and contrary to Section 3, the satisfaction of people's preferences does, as a matter of fact, promote their well-being (properly understood), simply because they know what they like. Bernheim (2016) makes something like this claim, invoking "the central Cartesian principle that subjective experience is inherently private and not directly observable." He adds: "We know how we feel; others can only make educated guesses. These considerations create a strong presumption in favor of deference to our judgments."

Bernheim (2016) also makes a separate argument, involving autonomy rather than welfare: "My views about my life are paramount because it is, after all, *my* life." This is a Kantian idea, suggesting the importance of respect for choosers, even if they err. People are ends, not means. Writing in this vein, Jeremy Waldron (2014) urges:

> Deeper even than this is a prickly concern about dignity. What becomes of the self-respect we invest in our own willed actions, flawed and misguided though they often are, when so many of our choices are manipulated to promote what someone else sees (perhaps rightly) as our best interest? ... I mean dignity in the sense of self-respect, an individual's awareness of her own worth as a chooser.

An emphasis on the idea that people are making choices about *their* lives might reflect a commitment to respect for dignity and autonomy, not welfare at all. That form of respect might stand as a decisive objection to paternalism in policy and law.

These arguments overlap with those in the canonical text on these questions, *On Liberty*, where Mill (2002) insisted:

> The only purpose for which power can be rightfully exercised over any member of a civilized community, against his will, is to prevent harm to others. His own good, either physical or moral, is not a sufficient warrant. He cannot rightfully be compelled to do or forbear because it will be better for him to do so, because it will make him happier, because, in the opinion of others, to do so would be wise, or even right.

Mill offered a number of separate justifications for his famous Harm Principle, but his most emphatic, and the most relevant here, is epistemic. It is in the same family as the first of Bernheim's: choosers are in the best position to know what is good for them. In Mill's view, the problem with outsiders, including government officials, is that they lack the necessary information. Mill insists that the individual "is the person most interested in his own well-being," and the "ordinary man or woman has means of knowledge immeasurably surpassing those that can be possessed by any one else." When society seeks to overrule the individual's judgment, it does so on the basis of "general presumptions," and these "may be altogether wrong, and even if right, are as likely as not to be misapplied to individual cases." If the goal is to ensure that people's lives go well, Mill concludes that the best solution is to allow people to find their own path.

That conclusion is echoed in Hayek's (2013) suggestion that "the awareness of our irremediable ignorance of most of what is known to somebody [who is a chooser] is *the chief basis of the argument for liberty*." For Hayek, the key contrast is between the chooser, who knows a great deal, and the outsiders, who show "irremediable ignorance," especially if they are social planners.

Much of the discussion here raises serious objections against these claims (again see Section 3). Nonetheless, some strands in contemporary behavioral welfare economics make elaborate and instructive arguments in Hayek's direction, suggesting that deference to individual choice is the right approach, subject to specific qualifications. Bernheim's emphasis on "the central Cartesian principle that subjective experience is inherently private and not directly observable," and on our unique knowledge of "how we feel," fits well with Mill's claim that the "ordinary man or woman has means of knowledge immeasurably surpassing those that can be possessed by anyone else." When people choose chocolate over vanilla, salmon over tuna, basketball over football, rest over recreation, or spending over saving, they do so because they know what they like. Outsiders are most unlikely to have that knowledge.

Once more, we should be cautious here. Return to the cases of Masters, Lancaster, Harston, and Ullner. It is true that even if people usually have unique knowledge of "how they feel," their knowledge on that count may not be perfect (Wilson, 2004). With respect to how choices will actually affect welfare, external observers might know far better, especially if the area requires technical expertise (Bubb and Pildes, 2014). Recall that choosers must solve a prediction problem; they must decide, at some point in advance of actual experience, about the effects of one or another option on experience (Kahneman et al., 1997; Sunstein, 2019b). To solve that problem, knowing "how they feel" is not enough. At a minimum, they must know "how they *will* feel," and they might not know nearly enough to know that. In many cases, most dramatically that of a pandemic, the case for a mandate may well turn out to be plausible on welfare grounds; return to the case of Ullner.

But as a general rule, the claim for the epistemic advantages of choosers is more than plausible. At the same time, it has taken a real battering from behavioral findings.

6 Judgments

Many people are troubled by that apparent battering (Allcott and Sunstein, 2015; Bernheim and Taubinsky, 2018; Goldin, 2017). Behavioral findings seem to suggest that "people do not reliably exercise good judgment." We have seen that people sometimes make mistakes about what would promote their own well-being, and in some cases, they are not the best judges of what would do that (Abaluck and Gruber, 2009, 2013; Afendulis et al., 2015; Bhargava et al., 2015, 2017). If so, Mill's epistemic argument is severely undermined. For purposes of law and policy, the door would seem open to paternalism, not only in the form of nudges but also in the form of mandates and bans (Conly, 2013; Bubb and Pildes, 2014). At least this is so if welfare is our guide.

Means Paternalism

In what might plausibly be taken as an effort to reconstruct and even to rescue the essentials of standard welfare economics and Mill's basic account, Bernheim (2016) responds that "the argument is faulty because it conflates what I will call direct and indirect judgments." In this way, Bernheim is attempting to lay the foundations for choice-oriented methods for welfare analysis in the presence of behavioral biases. In his account, a direct judgment involves ultimate objectives, or outcomes that people care about for their own sake. An indirect judgment involves alternatives that lead to those outcomes. We might understand direct judgments to involve intrinsic goods, and indirect judgments to involve goods that are instrumental to their realization.

As an example, Bernheim points to a person, called Norma, who is choosing between two boxes – a red one containing a pear and a yellow one containing an apple. She prefers apples, but she chooses the red one, mistakenly ending up with a pear. This is a welfare-reducing indirect judgment, and Bernheim agrees that Norma has made a mistake. More broadly: "Behavioral economics and psychology provide us with ample reason to question certain types of indirect judgments." In the face of a mistaken indirect judgment about money, safety, or health, a response might take the form of mandatory disclosure, or a warning, or perhaps some other nudge, such as a default rule; in extreme cases, it might justify a ban (Conly, 2013). But so long as we are speaking only of indirect judgments, we might insist that we have not departed radically from Mill's general framework, amending it only to say that for indirect judgments, his epistemic argument sometimes fails, perhaps because of reasoning failures of some kind or another (Le Grand and New, 2015). The cases of Marston, Lancaster, Harston, and Ullner can be understood in precisely these terms.

We can link Bernheim's (2016) argument here with the suggestion that findings in behavioral economics justify "means paternalism" but not necessarily "ends paternalism" (Le Grand and New, 2015; Sunstein, 2014). The basic idea is that people are sometimes mistaken about how to get to their own preferred destination. On that view, behaviorally informed interventions increase *navigability*, writ very large. A GPS device is a form of means paternalism; it allows drivers to specify where they want to go (and helps them get there). A default rule, automatically enrolling people in some program, can be seen as means paternalistic insofar as it is thought that (most) people prefer to be enrolled in that program (but do not enroll because they suffer from inertia; Madrian and O'Shea, 2002). A nutritional label can be seen as a form of means paternalism insofar as it improves people's ability to make their own choices about how to promote their ends (on the general subject, see Le Grand and New, 2015).

Many efforts to increase navigability, embodying a form of means paternalism, retain freedom of choice, and so can be seen as broadly compatible with Mill's Harm Principle (Sunstein, 2019a). But some do not. A ban on trans fats can be regarded as a form of means paternalism, at least if we are clear that the ban fits with, and does not undermine, people's ends (Conly, 2013). Occupational safety requirements can be seen in similar terms, even if they override the choices of unrealistically optimistic workers who would be willing to run the risks that those requirements eliminate (Akerlof and Dickens, 1982). Recall that when behavioral research finds that people are making a mistake, we have a behavioral market failure, in the sense that people's judgments lead to some kind of welfare loss, perhaps because of an identifiable behavioral bias (Bar-Gill, 2012; cf. Akerlof and Shiller, 2016). Much of behavioral law and economics is focused on that problem (Bar-Gill, 2012; Bubb and Pildes, 2014). As invoked for purposes of law and policy, behavioral market failures typically involve means paternalism (Le Grand and New, 2015; Bar-Gill, 2012). To see the underlying issues, let us use Bernheim's terminology, distinguishing between direct and indirect judgments.

Does that distinction work? How helpful is it? Insofar as we are dealing with unambiguously erroneous and unambiguously indirect judgments, and thus respecting people's ends, the problem of unjustified paternalism might seem to be solved. But when, in ordinary practice, are those involved in law or policy dealing with direct judgments? An initial problem is that if Norma prefers apples to pears, it is natural to ask whether an indirect judgment is involved as well. Apples are good, but it would be hard to justify the conclusion that they are "ultimate objectives, or outcomes that people care about for their own sake." (Friendship might be an intrinsic good – not so much apples.) If Norma prefers apples to pears, it is probably because she thinks that they taste better or perhaps that they are healthier. But perhaps she is wrong on either or both those counts.

In other words, her preference for apples is itself an indirect judgment, and she might be badly mistaken, perhaps because of behavioral bias.

As we have seen, the policy applications are numerous, including policy responses to unhealthy eating (Rabin, 2013), insufficient savings (Bubb and Pildes, 2014), and "dark patterns" online (Luguri and Strahilevitz, 2019). Bernheim (2016) is alert to this point and adds:

> Now let us add a wrinkle: assume Norma's ultimate goal is to achieve certain mental states ("internal goods"). From that perspective, all consumption items ("external goods") are means to ends, and choices among them always involve indirect judgments. Moreover, just as Norma may misjudge the contents of a box, she may also misapprehend the relationships between consumption goods and mental states. *However, assuming she is sufficiently familiar with apples, pears, and bananas to understand the consequences of eating each, her indirect judgments among open boxes will be correctly informed, and hence will faithfully reflect her direct judgments.*

What is rightly added here is more than a "wrinkle"; it is fundamental to behaviorally informed law and policy, and also to behavioral welfare economics. Norma is probably not concerned *only* with internal mental states (she might well care about price, health, and morality), and as we shall see, this is a significant point, counting against hedonic accounts of welfare; but when it comes to food choices, her mental state is almost certainly something that she cares about. Consumption choices are typically means to ends, and in that sense, they typically involve indirect judgments.

Moreover, the assumption of sufficient familiarity might not turn out to hold. For many choices, people are not sufficiently familiar with the options "to understand the consequences" of each, and even if they are, they might suffer from some kind of behavioral bias, such as present bias. Cigarette smoking is an example (Masiero et al., 2015). In this light, we should add that for Norma's choice of apples to be a good measure of her welfare, she must not only be informed ("sufficiently familiar") but also free from any such bias. Modifying Mill, we might adopt this working presumption in favor of an amended version of Premise 1, designed to orient behavioral welfare economics as applied to law and policy:

> *Working presumption: Each of us should be taken by outsiders to be the best judge of our own well-being, to the extent that we are adequately informed and sufficiently free of behavioral biases.*

The working presumption is an effort to build on choice-oriented methods for welfare analysis, as in Bernheim's approach, but for two reasons, it is more cautious. First, it is only a presumption. Second, it does not depend in any way on a distinction between direct and indirect judgments, or ends and means, though it is true that in application, it is usually likely to support interventions in the interest of means paternalism (Le Grand and New, 2015). Note also the words "should be taken by outsiders to be," as distinguished from the more dogmatic "are"; I return to the difference in the following discussion.

Of course, there are questions about how to operationalize the working presumption. If we care about welfare, it would make sense to examine what choices people make when they are actually well-informed; to see what choices people make when they do not suffer from limited attention and are in a position to evaluate all relevant facets of an option; to use people's active choices rather than passive ones, which may be a product of inertia; and to use otherwise unbiased choices, such as long-run choices based on a realistic understanding of facts, rather than biased ones, such as those that reflect present bias or optimistic bias (Allcott and Sunstein, 2015). Ideas of this kind can be seen as an effort to draw on a broadly Millian understanding, respectful of private choices, while also recognizing and giving weight to information deficits and behavioral biases.[2] They might provide a way to discipline behavioral welfare economics in areas that include savings behavior, decisions with respect to energy-efficient products, and choices of high-calorie or low-calorie food (Thunstrom, 2019).

By contrast, one of Bernheim's goals is to insist on respect for direct judgments. Instead of the working presumption immediately above, he argues in favor of two premises (Bernheim and Taubinsky, 2018):

Premise A: With respect to matters involving either direct judgment or correctly informed indirect judgment, each of us is the best arbiter of our own well-being.
Premise B: When we choose, we seek to benefit ourselves by selecting the alternative that, in our judgment, is most conducive to our well-being.

In defense of Premise A, Bernheim (2016) urges that existing economic research does not "provide evidence that people exercise poor direct judgment – for example, that they like certain goods or experiences 'too much' and others 'not enough.'" On the contrary, he maintains, "[t]he occasional objection to a direct judgment entails nothing more than a difference of opinion between the analyst and the consumer as to what constitutes a good or fulfilling life."

Differences of Opinion

The conclusion might be right, but these are strong words – too strong, in my view, and for three separate reasons. First, they disregard the possibility that people are genuinely making a mistake about what makes human lives go

---

[2] Akerlof and Shiller (2016) is in the same vein, though it emphasizes the active efforts by sellers to exploit those deficits and biases, or to "phish for" them.

well – not because of a mere difference of opinion between the analyst and the consumer but because that conclusion follows from *any* reasonable judgment about what it means for a human life to go well (cf. Acland, 2018). Second, they take a stand on some contentious philosophical issues about welfare (a point taken up as follows). Third, they collapse the distinction between two very different questions: (a) Do people know what they will like, before they have it? (b) Do people know what they like, when they are having it? Even if we think the answer to the second question is usually "yes," we have not answered the second question.

Repeating the basic claim elsewhere, Bernheim and Taubinsky add: "Thus there is no objective foundation for overturning the presumption in favor of a direct judgment and declaring the analyst's perspective superior" (Bernheim and Taubinsky, 2018). But the underlying issues are more complicated than that. It is true that if all we have is a "difference of opinion" between the analyst and the chooser, we do not, by stipulation, have an "objective foundation" for favoring the views of the analyst. But what if the analyst has actual data, suggesting that people's direct judgment produces large welfare losses (Levitt, 2016)? What if the analyst has information about what people are likely to like, and what if that information suggests that people's ex ante predictions are incorrect? What if the analyst has an account of what makes for a good or fulfilling life, not simply an "opinion" (Feldman, 2010)?

7 Theory and Practice

I now offer three general claims. The first is that for behaviorally informed law and policy, indirect judgments, or judgments about means, really are the coin of the realm. If we are speaking about inertia, present bias, unrealistic optimism, probability neglect (Sunstein, 2002), or limited attention, we are almost always dealing with judgments or decisions that might defeat people's own ends. And if we are speaking of default rules, disclosure, reminders, warnings, or uses of social norms, we are almost always dealing with efforts to encourage people to choose better means to achieve their own ends. Behavioral welfare economics typically deals with indirect judgments, and if it embraces paternalism, it is means paternalism (Le Grand and New, 2015).

The second is that with respect to direct judgments, behavioral welfare economics, like standard welfare economics, should proceed with humility. One reason is empirical; another is normative. To say that informed choosers are the best arbiters of their own welfare is to take a contested stand on how to think about the very idea of welfare. In the liberal tradition, time-honored ideas about autonomy and welfare do support a working presumption in favor of something like that proposition. But the presumption should be embraced with caution and with an understanding of what kind of stand it is taking.

The third claim, and the most ambitious, involves the proper understanding of welfare. Put too simply, the claim is that each of the three prevailing theories in philosophical circles – rooted in preferences, subjective well-being, and object-ive goods (Adler, 2011) – runs into serious problems. As we have seen, people's preferences, understood as their ex ante judgments about what to choose, will not always promote their welfare, simply because they might be inadequately informed or suffer from some kind of behavioral bias.

At the same time, we should not understand welfare in purely hedonic terms. People might choose to have a more meaningful life even if they end up sadder, more scared, or more anxious. They might care mostly about meaningfulness, not only about happiness or a lack of anxiety. For example, they might want to help others, especially the vulnerable; they might want to contribute to science or understanding; they might want to do something that they consider valuable or that connects with their deepest selves. People might choose a life that they consider to be better, even if they are more distressed as a result of choosing that life. These points might be taken to lead us to objective-good theories of well-being, and across a certain domain, those theories have considerable appeal. At the same time, what is good for John might not be good for Jane, and objective-good theories struggle (I suggest) to take account of heterogeneity.

The working presumption, sketched previously, is not meant to take a stand on the deepest philosophical questions; my hope is that it can be the outcome of an incompletely theorized agreement. But I shall try to bring the working presumption in contact with those questions and to show its appeal on prag-matic grounds. To simplify a complex story: The working presumption embodies an understanding that preference-based accounts of welfare must recognize that people might suffer from insufficient information and behav-ioral biases. The working presumption also recognizes that purely hedonic accounts of welfare, or those that focus on pleasures and pains and subjective well-being, miss the fact that reasonable people reasonably care about things other than their pleasures and their pains, their moods, their subjective well-being, or even their experiences. Recall that they might want to live meaning-ful lives. The working presumption is cautious about objective-good accounts of welfare, on the grounds that reasonable people choose to live a great diversity of good lives, but it leaves open the possibility that some lives are objectively bad or bad on any reasonable account of what matters to people (Acland, 2018).

Indirect Judgments Everywhere

As applied to law and policy (Thaler and Sunstein, 2008; Conly, 2013; Mullainathan and Shafir, 2013),[3] almost all of behavioral economics involves indirect judgments. The bulk of behavioral research involves such judgments as well (Kling et al., 2012). For example, the choice of one product over another – say, the Toyota RAV4 over the Toyota RAV4 Hybrid – will almost certainly be a result of a number of subsidiary judgments: how the preferred vehicle looks, how it drives, how reliable it will be, how big it is, the storage space, the purchase price, the anticipated cost of operation, how often one will have to go to a gas station and refuel. What is the direct judgment here?

We should agree that if a consumer named Susan makes some kind of clear mistake – she wants a smaller car and wrongly believes that the hybrid model is bigger – she is like Norma, selecting the wrong box. But suppose that Susan makes a subtler error: she is insufficiently responsive to fuel savings, in the sense that she would have saved a lot of money with the RAV4 Hybrid, but because of present bias, she decided against it (Gillingham et al., 2019). Unless we introduce other considerations (such as a liquidity constraint), Susan was mistaken. She was not, in this case, the best judge of her own well-being. Some kind of intervention would appear to be necessary, perhaps in the form of clear disclosure of relevant information (if the disclosure works, as it might not, to overcome present bias).

Perhaps we should say that Susan was not "sufficiently familiar with" the two kinds of cars "to understand the consequences" of choosing one or the other, and so her indirect judgment between the two was not "correctly informed, and hence" did not "faithfully reflect her direct judgments." Fair enough. But if that is the case, exactly how much remains of the idea of deference to individual judgment in cases of genuine or realistic interest to law and public policy?[4] A great deal still, perhaps, but a lot less than suggested by standard economic theory. In many circumstances, people are good indirect choosers, likely better than anyone else, but when they lack information or suffer from a behavioral bias, their indirect choices will not be reliable. Whether particular choices fall in that category is an empirical question.

---

[3] We can understand policy to include some behaviorally informed judgments of private institutions (Laibson, 2018).

[4] Recall Bernheim's acknowledgment of the possibility that "all consumption items ('external goods') are means to ends, and choices among them always involve indirect judgments." It is true that some governments impose coercive controls on intimate aspects of people's lives – as, for example, by criminalizing same-sex relations – and these controls might, at some point, be defended on behavioral grounds. But in the institutions that are now using behavioral economics, indirect judgments are the lay of the land, and the same is true of academic research that finds mistakes or recommends a behaviorally informed intervention.

To broaden the viewscreen, consider how many laws and regulations involve externalities, and for that reason, much of the welfare analysis need not draw on behavioral economics; it is conventional. For example, fuel economy regulations impose costs, which can be calculated (and which are imposed largely on consumers, in the form of higher sticker prices; Bento et al., 2019). Those regulations also reduce air pollution, including greenhouse gas emissions; monetization is more challenging here, but standard tools are available to do exactly that (Greenstone, 2013). To this extent, the welfare analysis should be familiar (Gayer and Viscusi, 2013). The distinctly behavioral dimension comes from possible errors on the part of consumers, who may not be giving sufficient weight to economic savings (from reduced gas usage) and also to time savings (from fewer visits to the gas station; see the catalog in Gayer and Viscusi, 2013). For behavioral reasons, consumers may indeed be making errors, which means that they stand to gain a great deal from fuel economy mandates, even when those mandates override their choices (for a skeptical view, see ibid.; for a less skeptical view, see Allcott and Sunstein, 2015).

Consumers can, of course, choose fuel-efficient vehicles if they like. If they do not, perhaps it is because the less fuel-efficient vehicles are smaller or less powerful, or because they are inferior along some other dimension. The behavioral question is whether consumers neglect fuel economy because of, for example, present bias, myopic loss aversion, or limited attention, or instead consider fuel economy but find it outweighed by other factors. The behavioral hunch is that present bias or limited attention does play a role, but a hunch is not evidence. Behavioral welfare economics would carefully investigate the hunch and consider consumer savings to the extent that the evidence suggests that they are real. In fact, that is a central, even defining, question in contemporary regulatory policy, bearing on energy efficiency requirements as well as fuel-economy regulation (Allcott and Knittel, 2019; Gillingham et al., 2019; Allcott and Sunstein, 2015; Gayer and Viscusi, 2013).

Defining Direct Judgments

What about people's direct judgments? Do they deserve deference? When? To make progress on these questions, we have to know how to identify them, which means that we have to solve what might be called the level of abstraction problem. Return to the case of Norma. We could say that she prefers Yellow Box to Red Box, believing that Yellow Box contains apples; that is clearly an indirect judgment because she wants an apple, not a pear. But we could also say that what she wants is a good snack rather than a less-good snack (bracketing the question of what, exactly, makes a snack good) and that the choice of an apple is an indirect judgment. Or we could say that what she wants is a good afternoon, or day, or year, or life, and the choice of a good snack is instrumental to one of those things.

Suppose that direct judgments are described at the highest level of abstraction – say, having a good life (without specifying what that means and on the assumption that a good life, properly defined, is intrinsically good). If so, essentially all real-world judgments are indirect judgments, in the sense that they are meant as ways of getting a good life. The problem is that if direct judgments are described at the highest levels of abstraction, and if the claim is that we must respect such judgments, outsiders (including regulators) are not much constrained even if they accept that claim. The reason is that outsiders (including regulators) are always, or almost always, dealing with indirect judgments, so long as direct judgments are taken at the highest levels of abstraction.

It would be possible to understand direct judgments at a lower level of abstraction. Choosers make judgments about what kind of day they want to have or what kind of life they want to lead. They might prefer high-calorie, full-sugar soda to diet drinks, or pizza to salad, even if they gain weight. They might like basketball but not football. They might want to devote themselves to family life. They might want to devote themselves to some cause. They might want to pursue art or sport. They might want to marry, or not. They might want to get drunk a fair bit, or not. They might want to live exciting, risk-filled lives, even at some cost to their health and longevity. Or they might want to live stable, risk-free lives, if that is the way to increase the number of years they have on the planet. Which of the resulting judgments is direct, and which is indirect? More fundamentally, does anything in behavioral science demonstrate that people are mistaken with respect to these judgments?

That is not the easiest question to answer. It is one thing to insist that people choose inferior health care plans, given their situations; that they make some bad food choices (Rabin, 2013), given their overall concerns; or that they do not purchase fuel-efficient motor vehicles when it would be in their economic interest to do so (Gillingham et al., 2019). It is quite another to insist that they choose the wrong sorts of days or lives. Do behavioral economists have anything to say on that question? If the answer is "yes," it might be for empirical reasons, and the problem may involve ends as well as means (Acland, 2018). As we saw in Section 3, a body of research in behavioral science points to "hedonic forecasting errors," which occur when people make mistaken predictions about the effects of outcomes or options on their subjective well-being (Gilbert, Gill, and Wilson, 1998; Gilbert and Wilson, 2000).

We have also seen that because the idea of "hedonic forecasting" is a bit narrow, we might ask whether people make "welfare forecasting errors" – that is, whether they make mistaken judgments about what will increase their welfare. They might think that their lives will be better if they marry, but they might be wrong. If so, we might be tempted to say that their judgment was indirect, which would bring us back to the level of abstraction problem. And if they are making the wrong choices, it probably must, simply as a logical matter, be because of a lack of information or some behavioral bias, though we might not be able to identify it, and though it might not be part of the standard catalog of behavioral biases (see the long catalog in Pohl, 2016).

8 Welfare

The largest question, of course, is how to define welfare. As noted, the philosophical literature distinguishes among three different theories: preference-based theories, hedonic theories, and objective-good theories (Adler, 2011). Economists are drawn to the former. As we have seen, they often speak in terms of allocative efficiency and some form of cost-benefit analysis, by which they explore potential Pareto improvements: Do the winners gain more than the losers lose? In principle, could the winners pay off the losers and leave some kind of surplus? To answer questions about allocative efficiency, economists often speak in terms of "willingness to pay." How much would people pay for reducing risks? There is an emerging literature on how to take account of behavioral findings in assessing allocative efficiency (Robinson and Hammitt, 2011; Weimer, 2017, 2020).

But if welfare in a broader sense is what matters, and if respect for preferences leads to welfare losses, such theories have real problems. If those problems lead us to embrace hedonic theories, emphasizing subjective well-being, we can make real progress in understanding the idea of forecasting errors. Recall that people might think that they would be happier in California and therefore move there, but perhaps they would not be happier at all (Schkade and Kahneman, 1998).[5] People might think that they would be unhappier if they left their current personal situation, but they might be quite mistaken on that point (Levitt, 2016).

What People Care About

Should we embrace hedonic theories? Many people think so. But such theories have serious limitations. I have already signaled some of them, but to be more concrete, consider some cases:

---

[5] Bernheim and Taubinsky (2018) raise a number of objections to reliance on subjective well-being. As noted, it is right to insist that subjective well-being is not the only thing that people care about; for example, choosers might sacrifice their subjective well-being for the sake of others, for the sake of living meaningful lives, or for the sake of moral goals. But the case for relying on choices, rather than subjective well-being, is not made out by that point. In some contexts, choices really are an effort to promote subjective well-being, and they go wrong.

1. John is deeply committed to public service; he wants to make the world better. He works long hours, and he does not especially enjoy it. His days are not a great deal of fun. But he does not want to do anything else.
2. Mary is a professional tennis player. She has been playing for most of her life. To her, tennis is not much fun. But she wants to pursue excellence. She aims to see how good she can get.
3. Frances is a lawyer. She is excellent at her job. She is an intense person. She likes winning; she finds it rewarding. But she also finds it stressful. She is not particularly happy.

These cases reflect what should be an obvious fact, which is that people care about things other than their hedonic state. To be sure, we could understand subjective well-being to include an array of values that go beyond hedonics; a sense of meaning, goodness, devotion, or excellence could be included in the catalog of what people care about. But if we do that, it is not clear that we are really speaking of *the quality of people's experiences*, which is often what is meant by subjective well-being. People care about things other than that quality. They might care about meaningfulness or excellence for their own sake, and not because they affect the quality of their experiences. They might choose options that do not improve their experiences but make for a worthier or more meaningful life. (Of course, it is true that a worthy life or a meaningful life might also have beneficial effects on people's experiences.)

It is for that reason that many people, including many economists, are drawn to preference-based theories, which can claim to take on board everything that people value, whether or not their experiences are improved. We have seen that preferences can go terribly wrong, in terms of what people care about, in the face of a lack of information or behavioral bias. But we can take that to be a friendly enough amendment to preference-based accounts. After all, it gives authority to (informed and unpolluted) preferences. As we have seen, one problem is that preference-based accounts pay too little attention to behavioral biases; perhaps that problem can be handled with suitable purification. But there is another problem, which is the risk that such accounts might pay too little attention to the ingredients of what is, for essentially all people, a good human life. If so, we might be drawn to objective-good accounts.

Such accounts take many forms. All of them would question the view that people's preferences deserve the kind of authority that many people, including many economists, would give them. Many philosophers embrace what they call "perfectionism," urging that some kinds of lives are simply better than others

(Hurka, 1996).[6] Some liberals are perfectionists; they give pride of place to a distinctive understanding of freedom (Raz, 1985). Some perfectionists are Aristotelian, emphasizing Aristotle's notion of functioning and an understanding of what it means for a human being to be truly human (Foot, 2001; Nussbaum, 1993, 2000). Marx was a perfectionist (Elster, 1985). Some forms of perfectionism have religious foundations; consider Aquinas.

On grounds of either autonomy (invoking Kant) or welfare (invoking Mill), we might want to reject perfectionism (Conly, 2013). But to say the least, these are complicated normative questions, and nothing in behavioral science, standard economics, or behavioral economics is equipped to solve them. It does seem reasonable to say that if preferences are an adaptation to injustice or acute deprivation, they do not deserve authority (Elster, 1983). In other words, some preferences do not have standing, a topic on which there is a large literature (ibid.; Whittington and McRae, 1986). It also seems reasonable to say that if people's preferences lead them to have objectively terrible lives, something has gone wrong. Objectively terrible lives might be painful, brutal, or short. Perhaps we can say that in such cases, people who choose such lives are almost certainly suffering from a lack of information or from a behavioral bias. But perhaps not; perhaps they prefer something that makes their lives painful, brutal, and short. It is in such cases that objective-good accounts have force.

This is not the place to try to answer some of the deepest questions. My main goal is to identify them. As John Rawls wrote in an unpublished manuscript, "We post a signpost. No deep thinking here; things are bad enough already." It makes pragmatic sense to say that across a wide range of choices, people's informed and unbiased preferences *generally* deserve authority because they are the best available reflection of what people actually care about. An important qualification arises when people's preferences lead them in directions that make their lives go less well (by their own lights). If they care about their own welfare, and if their choices compromise their welfare, there is a problem (Acland, 2018). Another qualification arises when their preferences lead them in the direction of what is, by any reasonable account, an objectively bad life. Because the range of objectively good or not-bad lives is (in my view) very wide, we should much hesitate before bringing that qualification into play. All this is enough, I hope, to support an incompletely theorized agreement on the working presumption, in the form of a willingness to embrace it even if we are puzzled or disagree about the largest questions.

---

[6] For a defense of liberal perfectionism, see Raz (1985); for critiques of perfectionism, see Rawls (1991) and Conly (2013). For a general account, see Zalta (2017).

9 Freedom

If we are concerned about human welfare, nudges have significant advantages over alternative approaches. If libertarian paternalists impose no material costs on those who seek to go their own way, then such approaches are less vulnerable to the (reasonable) objections that might be made against mandates and bans. The growing popularity of nudges attests to a mounting agreement on this point. Nonetheless, some people think that nudges are too intrusive and that they create serious risks (Glaeser, 2006). A full response to their objections would require many pages (Sunstein, 2019a; Sunstein, 2014b); I restrict myself to some brief remarks here.

Transparency and Manipulation

Mandates and commands are highly visible, and there is a good chance that the government will be held accountable for them. If public officials require increases in fuel economy, impose new energy efficiency requirements on refrigerators, forbid people from riding motorcycles without helmets, or require them to buckle their seat belts, nothing is mysterious, hidden, or secret. The prohibitions may or may not be acceptable, but they lack the distinctive vice of insidiousness. No one is confused or fooled. The government must defend itself publicly. And if the public defense is perceived as weak, the proposed action may well crumble. On this count, some people think that nudges do not fare so well (Glaeser, 2006). Some nudges might seem to be manipulative. Glaeser (2006) objects:

> Hard paternalism generally involves measurable instruments. The public can observe the size of sin taxes and voters can tell that certain activities have been outlawed. Rules can be set in advance about how far governments can go in pursuing their policies of hard paternalism. Effective soft paternalism must be situation-specific and creative in the language of its message. This fact makes soft paternalism intrinsically difficult to control and means that it is, at least on these grounds, more subject to abuse than hard paternalism.

The best response is simple. Nothing should be hidden, and everything should be transparent (Lades and Delaney, 2020; Le Grand and New, 2015). Indeed, transparency should be part of a kind of Bill of Rights for nudging (Sunstein and Reisch, 2019). Nudges should be visible, scrutinized, and monitored. Consider some of the initiatives discussed here: automatic enrollment in savings, health insurance, and school meal plans; the substitution of the Food Plate for the Food Pyramid; the revised fuel economy label; efforts to increase the salience of certain product attributes; and uses of social norms. All of these initiatives are visible, public, and entirely observable. All were, and remain, subject to public scrutiny. None is "intrinsically difficult to control." In this light, what is the problem?

Of Easy Reversibility

We have seen that in imposing very low costs, or in failing to impose material costs, on choices, nudges differ from mandates and bans. Because of the absence of such costs, nudges appear to be easily reversible, which is a strong point on their behalf. (I am speaking here of easy reversibility on the part of those who are nudged; of course, it is true that once a nudge is put in place by choice architects, it may or may not be easily reversible.)

For example, warnings do not override individual choice, and while they are not neutral and are meant to steer, people can ignore them if they want. We can easily imagine, and even find, warnings that are meant to discourage texting while driving, premarital sex, discrimination on the basis of sex, and gambling. However powerful, such warnings can be ignored. Those who run cafeterias and grocery stores might place fruits and vegetables in the front and cigarettes and fatty foods in the back. Even if so, people can always go to the back. A default rule in favor of automatic enrollment – in a savings or health insurance plan or a privacy policy – will greatly affect outcomes and may be decisive for many of us. But people can always opt out.

Does this mean that so long as a nudge is involved, no one should worry about paternalism, or indeed about any abuse of authority or power? That would be far too simple. Even when reversibility is easy in theory, it may prove unlikely in practice. In part because of the power of System 1, nudges may be decisive. True, we can search for chocolate candy and cigarettes at the back of the store, and true, we might opt out of health insurance (perhaps with a simple click) – but because of the power of inertia, many of us will not do so. The idea of easy reversibility might, in these circumstances, seem a bit of rhetoric, even a fraud – comforting, to be sure, but not a realistic response to those who are concerned about potential errors or bad faith on the part of nudgers.

It would be wrong to suggest that because of easy reversibility, all risks are eliminated. If people are defaulted into exploitative savings plans (with high fees and little diversification) or unduly expensive health insurance programs, it is not enough to say that they can go their own way if they choose to do so. If a website allows you to opt out of a privacy policy that permits it to track all of your movements on the Internet, you may say, "Yeah, whatever," and not alter the default. In view of the fact that people do not opt out even when it is easy to do so, a self-interested or malevolent government could easily nudge people in its preferred directions. If we accept very strong assumptions about the likelihood of government mistake and about the likely sense of private choice (uninfluenced by government), we might be cautious about official nudging – at least where it is not inevitable.

It remains true, however, that insofar as they maintain freedom of choice, nudges are less intrusive and less dangerous than mandates and bans. This is so even if people will exercise that freedom less often than they would if inertia and procrastination were not powerful forces. It is important to emphasize that in the face of bad defaults, a number of people will in fact opt out. For example, a study in the United Kingdom found that most people rejected a savings plan with an unusually high default contribution rate (12 percent of before-tax income; Beshears et al., 2010). Only about 25 percent of employees remained at that rate after a year, whereas about 60 of employees remained at a lower default contribution rate. A related finding is that workers were not much affected by a default allocation of a fraction of their tax refund to US savings bonds, apparently because such workers had definite plans to spend their refunds (Bronchetti et al., 2011).

The general lesson is that default rules will have a weaker effect, and potentially no effect, when the relevant population has a strong preference for a certain outcome. Nudges may fail – and that may well be good news. For that reason, liberty of choice is a real safeguard. We have seen enough to know that the freedom to opt out is no panacea. But it is exceedingly important.

Shoves

Some skeptics come from the opposite direction. In their view, nudges are not enough. Because people err, mandates are both desirable and necessary (Conly, 2013; Bubb and Pildes, 2014). On one view, decades of work in behavioral science have shown that choosers can go wrong. In this light, it might be asked: Is it not ironic, or worse, that a principal kind of behaviorally informed intervention places such a high premium on choice (Bubb and Pildes, 2014)? Why should behaviorally informed regulators emphasize freedom of choice when they know that people can err?

It is correct to say that if a mandate would increase social welfare, properly defined, there is a strong argument on its behalf. That is the test (for nudges as well as mandates). No one believes that nudges can solve the problem of violent crime. In the face of a standard market failure, coercion has a standard justification; consider the problem of air pollution. If people suffer from unrealistic optimism, limited attention, or a problem of self-control, and if the result is a serious welfare loss, there is an argument for some kind of public response, and it might take the form of a subsidy, a tax, or a ban (Farhi and Gabaix, 2020). We could certainly imagine cases in which the best approach is a mandate or a ban, because that response is preferable, from the standpoint of social welfare, to any alternative, including nudges. As we have seen, the best argument for subsidies, taxes, and bans might be behavioral in nature (Conly, 2013).

Nonetheless, there are many reasons to think that if improving social welfare is the goal, nudges have significant advantages and are often the best approach. It is a form of rhetoric to say that those who emphasize problems with choice should not be emphasizing the importance of choice. We might agree, for example, that people suffer from inertia, and that for that reason, they do not sign up for important programs and benefits. But if a default rule overcomes inertia, it is not ironic or paradoxical to think that those who choose to opt out may well be doing so for good reasons.

More generally, nudges might well have high benefits without high costs, and in any case, their net benefits may be higher than those of alternative approaches. Five points are especially important.

First, nudges make sense in the face of heterogeneity, at least in the sense that they can be preferable to mandates and bans. By allowing people to go their own way, they reduce the high costs potentially associated with one-size-fits-all solutions, which mandates often impose. Of course, it is also true that some nudges, such as default rules, may have disparate effects, some of them negative and some of them positive (Weimer, 2020; Bernheim et al., 2015). This is a point in favor of more personalized or targeted nudging. The only point is that nudges are more flexible than coercion.

Second, those who favor nudges are alert to the important fact that public officials have limited information and may themselves err (the knowledge problem). If nudges are based on mistakes, the damage is likely to be less severe than in the case of mandates, because nudges can be ignored or dismissed. Third, nudges respond to the fact that public officials may be improperly affected by the influence of well-organized private groups (the public choice problem). If so, the fact that people can go their own way provides an important safeguard, at least when compared with mandates. Fourth, nudges have the advantage of avoiding the welfare loss that people experience when they are deprived of the ability to choose. In some cases, that loss might be severe. Fifth, nudges recognize that freedom of choice can be seen, and often is seen, as an intrinsic good, which government should respect if it is to treat people with dignity.

To be sure, these points will have different degrees of force in different contexts. It is true that in the end, mandates might ultimately turn out to be justified on welfare grounds. But at least where harm to others is not involved, it makes sense to begin with less intrusive, choice-preserving alternatives and generally to adopt a (rebuttable) presumption in their favor. As we have seen, nudges are hardly the only tools in the toolbox of the behaviorally informed policy maker. But if we are trying to protect choosers from their own mistakes, they deserve pride of place.

10 Paths Forward

For behavioral science, there is a great deal more to learn. I have signaled that personalized or targeted nudges might be best. They can help those who would benefit from them and avoid hurting those who would not (Allcott and Kessler, 2019). This is one of the most important areas for welfare analysis in the future. It is also one of the most important areas for actual practice.

We also need to know much more about when nudges, or other behaviorally informed interventions, will have long-term rather than short-term effects. There is reason to think that default rules will be "sticky"; if people are automatically enrolled in some program, they might be there for a long time, possibly forever (Cronqvist et al., 2018). But for some nudges, including those that disclose information, the effects might be short-term, unless people are repeatedly exposed to that information (Allcott and Kessler, 2019). We need to know as well whether some behavioral interventions, including nudges, will produce compensating behavior or instead beneficial spillovers – as, for example, when a healthy meal at lunch leads to an unhealthy meal at dinner, or when a green nudge, with respect to some activity or behavior, leads to greener choices in other domains (Lanzini and Thøgersen, 2014).

But let us turn to the most fundamental points. In some cases, people lack information. In other cases, we can identify a behavioral market failure, in the sense that people fall prey to an identifiable behavioral bias and their choices make their lives go worse by their own lights. When this is so, some kind of corrective response is likely to be a good idea, perhaps in the form of a nudge, perhaps in the form of a tax, perhaps in the form of a mandate. In a free society, and notwithstanding the philosophical concerns, it nonetheless makes pragmatic sense for those involved in law and policy to adopt the working presumption. One more time:

> *Each of us should be taken to be the best judge of what will promote our own well-being, to the extent that we are adequately informed and sufficiently free of behavioral biases.*

In practice, that presumption can be disciplined by asking four subsidiary questions (Allcott and Sunstein, 2015):

1. *What do informed choosers choose?*
2. *What do active choosers choose?*
3. *In circumstances in which people are free of (say) present bias or unrealistic optimism, what do they choose?*
4. *What do people choose when their viewscreen is broad and they do not suffer from limited attention?*

Some of these subsidiary questions can be answered empirically. Consider, for example, the question whether and to what extent an absence of information leads consumers to fail to choose a fuel-efficient motor vehicle. Experiments might be designed to provide consumers with relevant information and see what they choose (Allcott and Knittel, 2019). The choices of informed consumers might be taken as the foundation for analysis. If most consumers make an active choice to enroll in overdraft protection programs under an opt-in regime, there is at least some reason to think that such programs are in their interests (Sarin, 2019). (Here I am bracketing the potential benefits of targeted or personalized programs.) Experiments might also be designed to make the potential economic savings of (say) energy-efficient light bulbs highly salient, at least potentially overcoming present bias and limited attention (Allcott and Taubinsky, 2015). If consumers choose or do not choose such light bulbs in such circumstances, we will have learned something about what is likely to increase their welfare – not everything, but something.

In principle, efforts to answer these subsidiary questions should help with cost-benefit analysis, where it is often challenging to know how to proceed when behavioral findings seem to cast doubt on standard uses of revealed preferences.[7] Answers to the subsidiary questions might also allow considerable room for regulatory interference with indirect judgments; such answers might well authorize means paternalism, often in the interest of overcoming reasoning failures or increasing navigability (Le Grand and New, 2015).

With respect to people's ends, operating at a high level of abstraction, those who offer the working presumption insist on considerable deference to freedom of choice. But they recognize that the underlying justifications for the presumption, founded on ideas about autonomy and welfare, cannot avoid taking some kind of philosophical stand. In some cases, ends paternalism might turn out to be justified, perhaps by reference to the same errors that justify means paternalism, and with reference to a relatively uncontroversial understanding of welfare,

---

[7] One example is the continuing dispute over the benefits, to consumers, of fuel economy and energy efficiency requirements (Allcott and Taubinsky, 2015). Another example is the dispute, also continuing, about how to value reductions in smoking: To what extent do such efforts improve the welfare of former smokers (Levy et al., 2018)? The framework introduced in Levy et al. (2018) is highly compatible with the analysis here.

focusing on what choosers themselves value (see Acland, 2018). Those who endorse the working presumption defend their position with conviction but also with humility. Recognizing that large questions can be found in the background and sometimes the foreground, they hope to achieve an incompletely theorized agreement on behalf of the presumption: an agreement among those who are uncertain about the most fundamental issues or who disagree intensely about how to resolve them.

In the end, we do well to adopt a presumption in favor of freedom of choice, with an understanding that what most matters is the kinds of lives that people are able to have, and with an insistence that freedom of choice is an important part of good lives. At its best, behavioral economics can help us to make freedom of choice real – and help people live lives that really are better, not least because they are longer.

References

Abaluck, J., & Gruber, J. (2009). Choice Inconsistencies among the Elderly. NBER Working Paper No. 14759. Available at www.nber.org/papers/w14759.

Abaluck, J., & Gruber, J. (2013). Evolving Choice Inconsistencies in Choice of Prescription Drug Insurance. NBER Working Paper No. 19163. Available at www.nber.org/papers/w19163.

Acland, D. (2018). The Case for Ends Paternalism: Extending Le Grand and New's Framework for Justification of Government Paternalism. *Review of Behavioral Economics*, 5(1), 1–22.

Adler, M. (2011). *Well-Being and Fair Distribution: Beyond Cost-Benefit Analysis*. Oxford: Oxford University Press.

Afendulis, C., Sinaiko, A. D., & Frank, R. G. (2015). Dominated Choices and Medicare Advantage Enrollment. *Journal of Economic Behavior and Organization*, 119(C), 72–83.

Affordable Care Act. 2010. The Patient Protection and Affordable Care Act of 2010. Pub. L. No. 111–148, 124 Stat. 119, codified in various sections of Title 42.

Agarwal, S., Chomsisengphet, S., Mahoney, N., & Stroebel, J. (2013). Regulating Consumer Financial Products: Evidence from Credit Cards. NBER Working Paper No. 19484.

Akerlof, G., & Dickens, W. (1982). The Economic Consequences of Cognitive Dissonance. *American Economic Review*, 72(3), 307–319.

Akerlof, G., & Shiller, R. (2016). *Phishing for Phools: The Economics of Manipulation and Deception*. Oxford: Oxford University Press.

Allcott, H. (2011a). Consumers' Perceptions and Misperceptions of Energy Costs. *American Economic Review*, 101, 98–104.

Allcott, H. (2011b). Social Norms and Energy Conservation. *Journal of Public Economics*, 95(9–10), 1082–1095.

Allcott, H. (2016). Paternalism and Energy Efficiency: An Overview. *Annual Review of Economics*, 8(1), 145–176.

Allcott, H., & Kessler, J. (2019). The Welfare Effects of Nudges: A Case Study of Energy Use Social Comparisons. *American Economic Journal: Applied Economics*, 11(1), 236–276.

Allcott, H., & Knittel, C. (2019). Are Consumers Poorly Informed about Fuel Economy? Evidence from Two Experiments. *American Economic Journal: Economic Policy*, 11(1), 1–37.

Allcott, H., Lockwood, B. B., & Taubinsky, D. (2019). Should We Tax Sugar-Sweetened Beverages? *Journal of Economic Perspectives*, 33(3), 202–227.

Allcott, H., & Sunstein, C. R. (2015). Regulating Internalities. *Journal of Policy Analysis and Management*, 34(3), 698–705.

Allcott, H., & Taubinsky, D. (2015). Evaluating Behaviorally Motivated Policy: Experimental Evidence from the Light Bulb Market. *American Economic Review*, 105(8), 2501–2538.

Bar-Gill, O. (2012). *Seduction by Contract: Law, Economics, and Psychology in Consumer Markets*. Oxford: Oxford University Press.

Behavioural Insights Team. (11 Apr 2014). EAST: Four Simple Ways to Apply Behavioural Insights. Available at www.bi.team/publications/east-four-simple-ways-to-apply-behavioural-insights/.

Benartzi, S., et al. (2017). Should Governments Invest More in Nudging? *Psychological Science*, 28(8), 1041–1055.

Benartzi, S., & Thaler, R. H. (2013). Behavioral Economics and the Retirement Savings Crisis. *Science*, 339(6124), 1152–1153.

Bento, A., Jacobsen, M. R., Knittel, C. R., & van Benthem, A. A. (2019). Estimating the Costs and Benefits of Fuel Economy Standards. NBER Working Paper No. 26309. Available at www.nber.org/papers/w26309.

Bernheim, B. D. (2009). Behavioral Welfare Economics. *Journal of the European Economic Association*, 7(2–3), 267–319.

Bernheim, B. D. (2016). The Good, the Bad, and the Ugly: A Unified Approach to Behavioral Welfare Economics. *Journal of Benefit-Cost Analysis*, 7(1), 12–68.

Bernheim, B. D., Fradkin, A., & Popov, I. (2015). The Welfare Economics of Default Options in 401(k) Plans. NBER Working Paper No. 17587.

Bernheim, B. D., & Rangel, A. (2007). Toward Choice-Theoretic Foundations for Behavioral Welfare Economics. *American Economic Review*, 97(2), 464–470.

Bernheim, B. D., & Rangel, A. (2009). Beyod Revealed Preference: Choice-Theoretic Foundations for Behavioral Welfare Economics. *The Quarterly Journal of Economics*, 124(1), 51–104.

Bernheim, B. D., & Taubinsky, D. (2018). Behavioral Public Economics. In Bernheim, B. D., DellaVigna, S., & Laibson, D. (eds.), *Handbook of Behavioral Economics: Foundation and Applications*, vol. 1, 381–516. Amsterdam: Elsevier.

Beshears, J., Choi, J., Laibson, D., & Madrian, B. (2010). The Limitations of Defaults. Unpublished manuscript. Retrieved from www.nber.org/programs/ag/rrc/NB10-02,%20Beshears,%20Choi,%20Laibson,%20Madrian.pdf.

Bettinger, E. P., Long, B. T., Oreopoulos, P., & Sanbonmatsu, L. (2009). The Role of Simplification and Information in College Decisions: Results from the H&R Block FAFSA Experiment. NBER Working Paper No. 15361. Available at www.nber.org/papers/w15361.

Bhargava, S., Loewenstein, G., & Sydnor, J. (2015). Do Individuals Make Sensible Health Insurance Decisions? Evidence from a Menu with Dominated Options. NBER Working Paper No. 21160. Available at www.nber.org/papers/w21160.

Bhargava, S., Loewenstein, G., & Sydnor, J. (2017). Choose to Lose: Health Plan Choices from a Menu with Dominated Option. *The Quarterly Journal of Economics*, 132(3), 1319–1372.

Bollinger, B., Leslie, P., & Sorenson, A. (2010). Calorie Labeling in Chain Restaurants. NBER Working Paper No. 15648. Available at www.nber.org/papers/w15648.

Bordalo, P., Gennaioli, N., & Shleifer, A. (2012a). Salience in Experimental Tests of the Endowment Effect. *American Economic Review*, 102(3), 47–52.

Bordalo, P., Gennaioli, N., & Shleifer, A. (2012b). Salience Theory of Choice Under Risk. *The Quarterly Journal of Economics*, 127(3), 1243–1285.

Bradley, S., & Feldman, N. (2020). Hidden Baggage: Behavioral Responses to Changes in Airline Ticket Tax Disclosure. *American Economic Journal: Economic Policy* (forthcoming).

Bronchetti, E. T., Dee, T. S., Huffman, D. B., & Magenheim, E. (2011). When a Nudge Isn't Enough: Defaults and Saving among Low-Income Tax Filers. NBER Working Paper No. 16887. Available at www.nber.org/papers/w16887.

Bronsteen, J., Buccafusco, C., & Masur, J. S. (2013). Well-Being Analysis vs. Cost-Benefit Analysis. *Duke Law Journal*, 62(8), 1603–1689.

Brown, J. R. (2007). Rational and Behavioral Perspectives on the Role of Annuities in Retirement Planning. NBER Working Paper No. 13537. Available at www.nber.org/papers/w13537.

Brown, J. R., Kling, J. R., Mullainathan, S., & Wrobel, M. V. (2008). Why Don't People Insure Late-Life Consumption? A Framing Explanation of the Under-Annuitization Puzzle. *American Economic Review*, 98, 304–09.

Bubb, R., & Pildes, R. (2014). How Behavioral Economics Trims Its Sails and Why. *Harvard Law Review*, 127(6), 1593–1678.

Cabinet Office (n.d.). The Behavioural Insights Team. Available at www.cabinetoffice.gov.uk/behavioural-insights-team.

Carroll, G. D., Choi, J. J., Laibson, D., Madrian, B. C., & Metrick, A. (2009). Optimal Defaults and Active Decisions. *The Quarterly Journal of Economics*, 124, 1639–74.

Centers for Medicare and Medicaid Services (February 4, 2010). Re: Express Lane Eligibility Option. Available at http://peerta.acf.hhs.gov/uploadedFiles/ Express%20Lane%20Eligibility%20SHO%20final%202-4-10%20508% 20ready.pdf.

Chetty, R., Friedman, J., Leth-Petersen, S., Nielsen, T., & Olsen, T. (2014). Active vs. Passive Decisions and Crowdout in Retirement Savings Accounts: Evidence from Denmark. *The Quarterly Journal of Economics*, 129(3), 1141–1219.

Chetty, R., Looney, A., & Kroft, K. (2009). Salience and Taxation: Theory and Evidence. *American Economic Review*, 99, 1145–1177.

Chiteji, N., & Walker, L. (2009). Strategies to Increase the Retirement Savings of African American Households. In Gale, W. G. et al. (ed.), *Automatic*, 231–260. Harrisburg: R. R. Donnelley.

CLASS Act 2010. Pub. L. No. 111–148, § 8, 124 Stat. 828, codified at 42 U.S.C. § 300 (2018).

Colin, M., O'Donoghue, T., & Vogelsang, T. (2004). Projection Bias in Catalogue Orders. Unpublished working paper. Cornell University Economics Department.

Conly, S. (2013). *Against Autonomy: Justifying Coercive Paternalism*. Cambridge: Cambridge University Press.

Credit Card Accountability Responsibility and Disclosure Act of 2009. Pub. L. No. 111–24, 123 Stat. 1734, codified in various sections of Titles 15 and 16.

Cronqvist, H., Thaler, R., & Yu, F. (2018). When Nudges Are Forever: Inertia in the Swedish Premium Pension Plan. *American Economic Review: Papers and Proceedings*, 108, 153–158.

DellaVigna, S., & Malmendier, U. (2006). Paying Not to Go to the Gym. *American Economic Review*, 96(3), 694–719.

Department of Agriculture. (2011). Direct Certification and Certification of Homeless, Migrant and Runaway Children for Free School Meals. 76 Fed. Reg. 22,785, 22,793.

Department of Education. (2010a). Program Integrity Issues, 75 Fed. Reg. 66,832, codified in various sections of Title 34 of the C.F.R.

Department of Education. (2010b). Department of Education Establishes New Student Aid Rules to Protect Borrowers and Taxpayers. Retrieved from www .ed.gov/news/press-releases/department-education-establishes-new-student-aid-rules-protect-borrowers-and-tax.

Department of the Treasury. (December 4, 2009). FinancialStability.gov TARP Transactions Data: Asset Guarantee Program. Retrieved from www.data.gov /raw/1260.

DG SANCO 2010. Consumer Affairs. Retrieved from http://ec.europa.eu/con sumers/docs/1dg-sanco-brochure-consumer-behaviour-final.pdf.

Dinner, I., Johnson, E. J., Goldstein, D. G., & Liu, K. (2011). Partitioning Default Effects: Why People Choose Not to Choose. *Journal of Experimental Psychology: Applied*, 17(4), 332.

Dodd-Frank Act 2010. 12 U.S.C. § 5511.

Dolan, P. (2014). *Happiness by Design: Change What You Do, Not How You Think*. New York: Penguin Group.

Downs, J. S., Loewenstein, G., & Wisdom, J. (2009). Strategies for Promoting Healthier Food Choices. *American Economic Review*, 99(2), 159–164.

Dunn, E. W., Gilbert, D. T., & Wilson, T. D. (2011). If Money Doesn't Make You Happy, Then You Probably Aren't Spending It Right. *Journal of Consumer Psychology*, 21(2), 115–125.

Ebeling, F., & Lotz, S. (2015). Domestic Uptake of Green Energy Promoted by Opt-Out Tariffs. *Nature Climate Change*, 5(9), 868–871.

Egebark, J., & Ekstrom, M. (2016). Can Indifference Make the World Greener? *Journal of Environmental Economics and Management*, 76, 1–13.

Elster, J. (1983). *Sour Grapes: Studies in the Subversion of Rationality*. Cambridge: Cambridge University Press.

Elster, J. (1985). *Making Sense of Marx*. Cambridge: Cambridge University Press.

Emergency Planning and Community Right to Know Act 1986. Pub. L. No. 99–499, 100 Stat. 1728, codified at 42 USC § 11001 *et seq*.

Environmental Protection Agency. (2009). Fuel Economy Labeling of Motor Vehicles: Revisions to Improve Calculation of Fuel Economy Estimates. 74 Fed. Reg. 61,537, 61,542, 61,550–53 (amending 40 C.F.R. Parts 86,600).

European Commission. (2012). Science for Environment Policy, Future Brief: Green Behavior. Retrieved from http://ec.europa.eu/environment/integra tion/research/newsalert/pdf/FB4.pdf.

Executive Order 13563: Improving Regulation and Regulatory Review. (2011). 76 Fed. Reg. 3821.

Executive Order 13707: Using Behavioral Science Insights to Better Serve the American People. (2015). 80 Fed. Reg. 56,365.

Farhi, E., & Gabaix, X. (2020). Optimal Taxation with Behavioral Agents. *American Economic Review*, 110(1), 298–336.

Feldman, F. (2010). *What Is This Thing Called Happiness?* Oxford: Oxford University Press.

Finkelstein, A. (2009). E-ZTAX: Tax Salience and Tax Rates. *The Quarterly Journal of Economics*, 124, 969–1010.

Food and Drug Administration. (2014). Regulatory Impact Analysis for Final Rules on "Food Labeling: Revision of the Nutrition and Supplement Facts Labels." Available at https://www.fda.gov/media/98712/download.

Foot, P. (2001). *Natural Goodness*. Oxford: Clarendon Press.

Gabaix, X. (2019). Behavioral Inattention. NBER Working Paper No. 24096.

Gabaix, X., & Laibson, D. (2006). Shrouded Attributes, Consumer Myopia, and Information Suppression in Competitive Markets. *Quarterly Journal of Economics*, 121(2), 505–540.

Gale, W., Iwry, J., & Walters, S. (2009). Retirement Savings for Middle- and Lower-Income Households: The Pension Protection Act of 2006 and the Unfinished Agenda. In Gale, W. G. et al. (eds.), *Automatic* (11–27), Harrisburg: R. R. Donnelley.

Gayer, T., & Viscusi, W. K. (2013). Overriding Consumer Preferences with Energy Regulations. *Journal of Regulatory Economics*, 43(3), 248–264.

Gilbert, D. T., Gill, M. J., & Wilson, T. D. (1998). How Do We Know What We Will Like? The Informational Basis of Affective Forecasting. Unpublished manuscript. Harvard University.

Gilbert, D., Pinel, E. C., Wilson, T. D., Blumberg, S. J., & Wheatley, T. P. (1998). Immune Neglect: A Source of Durability Bias in Affective Forecasting. *Journal of Personality and Social Psychology*, 75(3), 617–638.

Gilbert, D., & Wilson, T. (2000). Miswanting: Some Problems in the Forecasting of Future Affective States. In Forgas, J. P. (ed.), *Feeling and Thinking: The Role of Affect in Social Cognition*. Cambridge: Cambridge University Press.

Gillingham, K., Houde, S., & van Benthem, A. A. (2019). Consumer Myopia in Vehicle Purchases. NBER Working Paper No. 25845. Available at www.nber.org/papers/w25845.

Glaeser, E. (2006). Paternalism and Psychology. *University of Chicago Law Review*, 73(1), 133–156.

Goldin, J. (2015). Which Way to Nudge? Uncovering Preferences in the Behavioral Age. *Yale Law Journal*, 125(1), 226–270.

Goldin, J. (2017). Libertarian Quasi-Paternalism. *Missouri Law Review*, 82, 669–682.

Greenstone, M. (2013). Developing a Social Cost of Carbon for US Regulatory Analysis. *Review of Environmental Economics and Policy*, 7(1), 23–46.

GreeNudge.org. (2018). Frontpage. Available at https://greenudge.org/.

Gruber, J., & Abaluck, J. T. (2011). Choice Inconsistencies among the Elderly: Evidence from Plan Choice in the Medicare Part D Program. *American Economic Review*, 101, 1180–1210.

Gruber, J., & Mullainathan, S. (2005). Do Cigarettes Taxes Make Smokers Better Off? *The B.E. Journal of Economic Analysis & Policy*, 5(1), 1–45.

Gul, F., & Pesendorfer, W. (2004). Self-Control, Revealed Preference and Consumption Choice. *Review of Economic Dynamics*, 7(2), 243–264.

Halpern, D. (2015). *Inside the Nudge Unit: How Small Changes Can Make a Big Difference*. New York: Random House.

Hausman, D., & McPherson, M. (2009). Preference Satisfaction and Welfare Economics. *Economics and Philosophy*, 25, 1–25.

Hayek, F. (2013). The Market and Other Orders. In Caldwell, B. (ed.), *The Collected Works of F. A. Hayek*. Chicago: University of Chicago Press.

Healthy, Hunger–Free Kids Act 2012. Pub. L. No. 111–296, 124 Stat. 3183.

Heath, C., & Heath, D. (2010). *Switch: How to Change Things When Change Is Hard*. New York: Broadway.

Homonoff, T. (2018). Can Small Incentives Have Large Effects? The Impact of Taxes Versus Bonuses on Disposable Bag Use. *American Economic Journal: Economic Policy*, 10(4), 177–210.

Howarth, R. B., Haddad, B. M., & Paton, B. (2000). The Economics of Energy Efficiency: Insights from Voluntary Participation Programs. *Energy Policy*, 28, 477–486.

Hsee, C. (2000). Attribute Evaluability and its Implications for Joint-Separate Evaluation Reversals and Beyond. In Kahneman, D., & Tversky, A. (eds.), *Choices, Values and Frames*. Cambridge: Cambridge University Press.

Hurka, T. (1996). *Perfectionism*. Oxford: Oxford University Press.

Internal Revenue Service. (September 2009). Retirement and Savings Initiatives: Helping Americans Save for the Future. Retrieved from www.irs.gov/pub/irs-tege/rne_se0909.pdf.

iNudgeYou.com. (n.d.). Resources. Retrieved from www.inudgeyou.com/resources.

Jachimowicz, J., Duncan, S., Weber, E. U., & Johnson, E. J. (2019). Why and When Defaults Influence Decisions: A Meta-Analysis of Default Effects. *Behavioral Public Policy*, 3(2), 159–186.

Johnson, E., & Goldstein, D. (2013). Decisions by Default. In Shafir, E. (ed.), *The Behavioral Foundations of Public Policy*, 417–427. Princeton: Princeton University Press.

Iyengar, S., & Kamenica, E. (2010). Choice Proliferation, Simplicity Seeking, and Asset Allocation. *Journal of Public Economics*, 94, 530–39.

Kahneman, D. (2011). *Thinking, Fast and Slow*. New York: Farrar, Straus, and Giroux.

Kahneman, D., & Frederick, S. (2002). Representativeness Revisited: Attribute Substitution in Intuitive Judgment. In Gilovich, T., Griffin, D., & Kahneman, D. (eds.), *Heuristics and Biases*, 49–81. Cambridge: Cambridge University Press.

Kahneman, D., Fredrickson, B. L., Schreiber, C. A., & Redelmeier, D. A. (1993). When More Pain Is Preferred to Less: Adding a Better End. *Psychological Science*, 4(6), 401–405.

Kahneman, D., Wakker, P. P., & Sarin, R. (1997). Back to Bentham? Explorations of Experienced Utility. *The Quarterly Journal of Economics*, 112(2), 375–405.

Kaiser, M., Bernauer, M., Sunstein, C. R., & Reisch, L. A. (2020). The Power of Green Defaults: The Impact of Regional Variation of Opt-Out Tariffs on Green Energy Demand in Germany. *Ecological Economics*, 174, 106685.

Kamenica, E., Mullainathan, S., & Thaler, R. (2011). Helping Consumers Know Themselves. *American Economic Review*, 101(3), 417–422.

Keren, G. (ed.). (2011). *Perspectives on Framing*. New York: Society for Judgment and Decision Making.

Kling, J., Mullainathan, S., Shafir, E., Vermeulen, L., & Wrobel, M. V. (2012). Comparison Friction: Experimental Evidence from Medicare Drug Plans. *The Quarterly Journal of Economics*, 127(1), 199–235.

Korobkin, R. B. (2013). Relative Value Health Insurance: The Behavioral Law and Economics Solution to the Health Care Cost Crisis. *Journal of Scholarly Perspectives*, 10(1), 51–68.

Kronlund, M., Pool, V., Sialm, C., & Stefanesco, I. (2020). Out of Sight No More? The Effect of Fee Disclosures on 401K Investment Allocations. NBER Working Paper No. 27573. Available at www.nber.org/papers/w27573.

Lades, L. K., & Delaney, L. (2020). Nudge FORGOOD. *Behavioural Public Policy*, 1–20. Available at DOI:10.1017/bpp.2019.53.

Laibson, D. (1997). Golden Eggs and Hyperbolic Discounting. *The Quarterly Journal of Economics*, 112(2), 443–478.

Laibson, D. 2018. Private Paternalism, the Commitment Puzzle, and Model-Free Equilibrium. *AEA Papers and Proceedings*, 108, 1–21.

Lanzini, P., & Thøgersen, J. (2014). Behavioral Spillover in Environmental Domain: An Intervention Study. *Journal of Environmental Psychology*, 40, 381–390.

Le Grand, J., & New, B. (2015). *Government Paternalism: Nanny State or Helpful Friend?* Princeton: Princeton University Press.

Levitt, S. (2016). Heads or Tails: The Impact of a Coin Toss on Major Life Decisions and Subsequent Happiness. NBER Working Paper No. 22487. Available at www.nber.org/papers/w22487.

Levy, H. G., Norton, E. C., & Smith, J. A. (2018). Tobacco Regulation and Consumer Surplus: How Should We Value Foregone Consumer Surplus? *American Journal of Health Economics*, 4(1), 1–25.

Loewenstein, G. (2005). Hot-Cold Empathy Gaps and Medical Decision Making. *Health Psychology*, 24(4S), S49.

Loewenstein, G., O'Donoghue, T., & Rabin, M. (2003). Projection Bias in Predicting Future Utility. *The Quarterly Journal of Economics*, 118(4), 1209–1248.

Luguri, J., & Strahilevitz, L. (2019). Shining a Light on Dark Patterns. University of Chicago, Public Law Working Paper No. 719. Available at https://papers.ssrn.com/sol3/papers.cfm?abstract_id=3431205.

Madrian, B. C., & Shea, D. (2002). The Power of Suggestion: Inertia in 401(k) Participation and Savings Behavior. *The Quarterly Journal of Economics*, 116(4), 1149–1187.

Masiero, M., Lucchiari, C., & Pravettoni, G. (2015). Personal Fable: Optimistic Bias in Cigarette Smokers. *International Journal of High Risk Behaviors & Addiction*, 4(1), e20939.

Mattauch, L., & Hepburn, C. (2016). Climate Policy When Preferences Are Endogenous – and Sometimes They Are. *Midwest Studies in Philosophy*, 40 (1), 76–95.

Mill, J. S. (2002). On Liberty. In Miller, D. E. (eds.), *The Basic Writings of John Stuart Mill: On Liberty, The Subjection of Women, and Utilitarianism*, 3, 11–12. New York: Random House.

Morewedge, C. K., Gilbert, D. T., Myrseth, K. O. R., Kassam, K. S., & Wilson, T. D. (2010). Consuming Experience: Why Affective Forecasters Overestimate Comparative Value. *Journal of Experimental Social Psychology*, 46(6), 986–992.

Mullainathan, S., & Shafir, E. (2013). *Scarcity: Why Having Too Little Means So Much*. New York: Times Books.

Mulligan, J. (January 26, 2011). First Lady Michelle Obama Announces Collaboration with Walmart in Support of Let's Move Campaign. Retrieved from www.letsmove.gov/blog/2011/01/25/first-lady-michelle-obama-announces-collaboration-walmart-support-lets-move-campaign.

Nisbett, R. E., & Kanouse, D. E. (1968). Obesity, Hunger, and Supermarket Shopping Behavior. In *Proceedings of the Annual Convention of the American Psychological Association*. New York: American Psychological Association.

Nussbaum, M. C. (1993). Non-Relative Virtues: An Aristotelian Approach. In Nussbaum, M. C., & Sen, A. (eds.), *The Quality of Life*. Oxford: Clarendon Press.

Nussbaum, M. C. (2000). *Women and Human Development: The Capabilities Approach*. Cambridge: Cambridge University Press.

Obama, B. (September 5, 2009). Weekly Address.

O'Donoghue, T., & Rabin, M. (2001). Choice and Procrastination. *The Quarterly Journal of Economics*, 116(1), 121–160.

O'Donoghue, T., & Rabin, M. (2015). Present Bias: Lessons Learned and to Be Learned. *American Economic Review*, 105(5), 273–279.

Organisation for Economic Cooperation and Development. (2010). Consumer Policy Toolkit. Retrieved from www.oecd.org/sti/consumerpolicy/consumer policytoolkit.htm.

Orszag, P. R. (March 29, 2010). OMB, Director, SAVEings. Retrieved from www.whitehouse.gov/omb/blog/10/03/29/SAVEings/.

Orszag, P. R., & Rodriguez, E. (2009). Retirement Security for Latinos: Bolstering Coverage, Savings, and Adequacy. In Gale, W. G. et al. (ed.), *Automatic*, 173–98. Harrisburg: R. R. Donnelley.

Papke, L. E., Walker, L., & Dworsky, M. (2009). Retirement Savings for Women: Progress to Date and Policies for Tomorrow. In Gale, W. G. et al. (ed.), *Automatic*, 199–230. Harrisburg: R. R. Donnelley.

Pension Protection Act 2006. Pub. L. No. 109–280, 120 Stat. 780, codified in various sections of Titles 26 and 29.

Pettigrew, R. (2020). *Choosing for Changing Selves*. Oxford: Oxford University Press.

Pichert, D., & Katsikopoulos, K. V. (2008). Green Defaults: Information Presentation and Pro-Environmental Behaviour. *Journal of Environmental Psychology*, 28(1), 63–73.

Pohl, R. F. (ed.). (2016). *Cognitive Illusions*. Abingdon: Routledge Company.

Posner, R. (1973). *Economic Analysis of Law*. New York: Wolters Kluwer Law & Business.

Rabin, M. (2013). Healthy Habits: Some Thoughts on the Role of Public Policy in Healthful Eating and Exercise Under Limited Rationality. In Oliver, A. (ed.), *Behavioral Public Policy*. Cambridge: Cambridge University Press.

Rawls, J. (1991). Political Liberalism. In Levy, Jacob T. (ed.), *Oxford Handbook of Classics in Contemporary Political Theory*. Oxford: Oxford University Press.

Raz, J. (1985). *The Morality of Freedom*. Oxford: Oxford University Press.

Read, D., Antonides, G., van den Ouden, L., & Trienekens, H. (2001). Which is Better: Simultaneous or Sequential Choice? *Organizational Behavior and Human Decision Processes*, 84(1), 54–70.

Read, D., Loewenstein, G., & Kalyanaraman, S. (1999). Mixing Virtue and Vice: Combining the Immediacy Effect and the Diversification Heuristic. *Journal of Behavioral Decision Making*, 12(4), 257–273.

Redelmeier, D. A., Katz, J., & Kahneman, D. (2003). Memories of Colonoscopy: A Randomized Trial. *Pain*, 104(1–2), 187–194.

Riis, J., & Ratner, R. (2015). Simplified Nutrition Guidelines to Fight Obesity. In Batra, R., Keller, P. A., & Strecher, V. J. (eds.), *Leveraging Consumer Psychology for Effective Health Communications: The Obesity Challenge*. Armonk, NY: M. E. Sharpe.

Robinson, L. A., & Hammitt, J. K. (2011). Behavioral Economics and the Conduct of Benefit-Cost Analysis: Towards Principles and Standards. *Journal of Benefit-Cost Analysis*, 2(2), 1–51.

Sahm, C. R., Shapiro, M. D., & Slemrod, J. (2011). Check in the Mail or More in the Paycheck: Does the Effectiveness of Fiscal Stimulus Depend on How It Is Delivered? Finance and Economics Discussion Series No. 2010–40. Available at www.federalreserve.gov/pubs/feds/2010/201040/201040pap.pdf.

Sarin, N. (2019). Making Consumer Finance Work. *Columbia Law Review*, 119 (6), 1519–1596.

Schreiber, C. A., & Kahneman, D. (2000). Determinants of the Remembered Utility of Aversive Sounds. *Journal of Experimental Psychology: General*, 129(1), 27.

Schkade, D., & Kahneman, D. (1998). Does Living in California Make People Happy? A Focusing Illusion in Judgments of Life Satisfaction. *Psychological Science*, 9(5), 340–346.

Scholten, M., Read, D., & Stewart, N. (2019). The Framing of Nothing and the Psychology of Choice. *Journal of Risk and Uncertainty*, 59, 125–149.

Sethi-Iyengar, S., Huberman, G., & Jiang, W. (2004). How Much Choice is Too Much? Contributions to 401(k) Retirement Plans. In Mitchell, O. S., & Utkus, S. P. (eds.), *Pension Design and Structure: New Lessons from Behavioral Finance*. Oxford:Oxford University Press.

Sharot, T. (2011). *The Optimism Bias: A Tour of the Irrationally Positive Brain*. New York: Knopf Publishing.

Simonson, I. (1990). The Effect of Purchase Quantity and Timing on Variety-Seeking Behavior. *Journal of Marketing Research*, 27(2), 150–162.

Sparkman, G., & Walton, G. M. (2017). Dynamic Norms Promote Sustainable Behavior, Even If It Is Counternormative. *Psychological Science*, 28(11), 1663–1674.

Sugden, R. (2018). "Better Off, as Judged by Themselves": A Reply to Cass Sunstein. *International Review of Economics*, 65(1), 9–13. Available at https://doi.org/10.1007/s12232-017-0281-8.

Sunstein, C. R. (2002). Probability Neglect. *Yale Law Journal*, 112(1), 61–107.

Sunstein, C. R. (2011). Empirically Informed Regulation. *University of Chicago Law Review*, 78, 1349–1429.

Sunstein, C. R. (2013). *Simpler*. New York: Simon and Schuster.

Sunstein, C. R. (2014). *Why Nudge? The Politics of Libertarian Paternalism*. New Haven: Yale University Press.

Sunstein, C. R. (2018a). *Legal Reasoning and Political Conflict*. Oxford: Oxford University Press.

Sunstein, C. R. (2018b). On Preferring A to B, While also Preferring B to A. *Rationality and Society*, 30(3), 305–331.

Sunstein, C. R. (2019a). *On Freedom*. Princeton: Princeton University Press.

Sunstein, C. R. (2019b). Rear Visibility and Some Unresolved Problems for Economic Analysis. *Journal of Benefit-Cost Analysis*, 10(3), 317–350.

Sunstein, C. R. (2019c). Ruining Popcorn? The Welfare Effects of Information. *Journal of Risk and Uncertainty*, 58, 121–142.

Sunstein, C.R. (2019d). Sludge and Ordeals. *Duke Law Journal*, 68, 1843–1883.

Sunstein, C. R. (2020). *Too Much Information*. Cambridge: MIT Press.

Sunstein, C. R., & Reisch, L. A. (2014). Automatically Green: Behavioral Economics and Environmental Protection. *Harvard Environmental Law Review*, 38, 127–158.

Sunstein, C. R. & Reisch, L. A. (2019). *Trusting Nudges: Toward A Bill of Rights for Nudging*. London: Routledge.

Thaler, R. (2015). *Misbehaving: The Making of Behavioral Economics*. New York: W. W. Norton & Co.

Thaler, R. H., & Benartzi, S. (2004). Save More Tomorrow™: Using Behavioral Economics to Increase Employee Saving. *Journal of Political Economy*, 112(S1), S164–S187.

Thaler, R. H., & Sunstein, C. R. (2008). *Nudge: Improving Decisions about Health, Wealth, and Happiness*. New Haven: Yale University Press.

Thunstrom, L. (2019). Welfare Effects of Nudges: The Emotional Tax of Calorie Menu Labeling. *Judgment and Decision Making*, 14(1), 11–25.

Turnwald, B. P., et al. (2019). Increasing Vegetable Intake by Emphasizing Tasty and Enjoyable Attributes: A Randomized Controlled Multisite Intervention for Taste-Focused Labeling. *Psychological Science*, 30(11), 1603–1615.

Ubel, P. A., Loewenstein, G., Schwarz, N., & Smith, D. (2005). Misimagining the Unimaginable: The Disability Paradox and Health Care Decision Making. *Health Psychology*, 24(4S), S57.

Ullmann-Margalit, E. (2006). Big Decisions: Opting, Converting, and Drifting. *Royal Institute of Philosophy Supplement*, 58, 157–172.

Waldron, J. (2014). It's All for Your Own Good. Available at www.nybooks.com /articles/archives/2014/oct/09/cass-sunstein-its-all-your-own-good/.

Weimer, D. L. (2017). *Behavioral Economics for Cost-Benefit Analysis: Benefit Validity When Sovereign Consumers Seem to Make Mistakes*. Cambridge: Cambridge University Press.

Weimer, D. L. (2020). When Are Nudges Desirable? Benefit Validity When Preferences Are Not Consistently Revealed. *Public Administration Review*, 80(1), 118–126.

Whittington, D., & MacRae Jr., D. (1986). The Issue of Standing in Cost-Benefit Analysis. *Journal of Policy Analysis and Management*, 5(4), 665–682.

Willis, L. E. (2013). When Nudges Fail: Slippery Defaults. *The University of Chicago Law Review*, 80(3), 1155–1229.

Wilson, T. (2004). *Strangers to Ourselves: Discovering the Adaptive Unconscious*. Cambridge, MA: Belknap Press.

Wilson, T. D., & Gilbert, D. T. (2003). Affective Forecasting. *Advances in Experimental Social Psychology*, 35, 345–411.

Zalta, E. N. (ed.). (2017). Perfectionism in Moral and Political Philosophy. *Stanford Encyclopedia of Philosophy*. Available at https://plato.stanford.edu /entries/perfectionism-moral/.

Zywicki, T. J. (2013). The Economics and Regulation of Bank Overdraft Protection. George Mason University Law & Economics Research Paper No. 11–43. Available at http://papers.ssrn.com/sol3/papers.cfm? abstract_id=1946387.

9 C.F.R. § 317.309.

12 C.F.R. § 205.17.

29 C.F.R. §§ 2550.404a-5.

34 C.F.R. § 668.6.

Acknowledgments

Thanks above all to Daniel Kahneman and Richard Thaler, beloved friends and coauthors from whom I have learned so much. Section 3 of this Element, on whether people's choices make them happy, was originally coauthored with Thaler and intended as a chapter in our book *Nudge*. It was one of several chapters that did not make the final cut – in this case, because it would disrupt the flow. Thaler deserves all credit for whatever is good in that section and no blame for whatever is not. (The choice to include it here makes me happy.)

I am also grateful to Matthew Adler, Hunt Allcott, Oren Bar-Gill, Thomas Kneisner, David Strauss, Dmitri Taubinsky, and W. Kip Viscusi for exceptionally valuable comments on a portion of the manuscript. Several projects with Edna Ullmann-Margalit provided the foundations for some of what is here. Three anonymous reviewers provided extremely helpful comments. Lia Cattaneo, Dinis Cheian, Royit Goyal, and Eli Nachmany provided superb research assistance and excellent suggestions. Parts of this book draw on my essay, "Behavioral Welfare Economics," *Journal of Benefit-Cost Analysis*, 11, 196 (2020), and I am grateful to Cambridge University Press for permission to use and adapt that material here.

Cambridge Elements

Public Economics

Robin Boadway

Queen's University

Robin Boadway is Emeritus Professor of Economics at Queen's University. His main research interests are in public economics, welfare economics and fiscal federalism.

Frank A. Cowell

The London School of Economics and Political Science

Frank A. Cowell is Professor of Economics at the London School of Economics. His main research interests are in inequality, mobility and the distribution of income and wealth.

Massimo Florio

University of Milan

Massimo Florio is Professor of Public Economics at the University of Milan. His main interests are in cost-benefit analysis, regional policy, privatization, public enterprise, network industries and the socio-economic impact of research infrastructures.

About the Series

The Cambridge Elements of Public Economics provides authoritative and up-to-date reviews of core topics and recent developments in the field. It includes state-of-the-art contributions on all areas in the field. The editors are particularly interested in the new frontiers of quantitative methods in public economics, experimental approaches, behavioral public finance, empirical and theoretical analysis of the quality of government and institutions.

Cambridge Elements ≡

Public Economics

Printed in the United States
By Bookmasters